MW00448333

"As the church in the West once again faces the prospect of being a 'little flock' surrounded by an increasingly hostile post-Christian culture, it is not surprising that some of the main features of the life of the early church should reappear that until recently didn't seem either relevant or realistic. Texts of the Scripture and main aspects of Jesus' ministry that were consigned to another age are beginning to be seen as extremely relevant once again. Thelen has done the church a great service by establishing the solid scriptural and theological foundations for the place of 'signs and wonders' in the mission of the church today."

—**RALPH MARTIN**
Director, Sacred Heart Major Seminary, Archdiocese of Detroit

"Thelen gives us a convincing and forceful explanation of the evangelistic impact of Jesus' miraculous healing ministry and its continuation in the life of his disciples. By a thorough examination of the biblical text with recourse to the best current scholarship, he firmly grounds the practice of Christian healing in the New Testament narratives and letters of St. Paul. Based on his exegesis, he argues compellingly that the signs and wonders of Jesus and his disciples not only attest to his messianic identity but also are closely linked to the effective proclamation of the gospel. Essentially, miraculous healing leads people to be open to the gospel. He demonstrates the unique significance of divine healing for the evangelization of a postmodern culture and issues a stirring call for Christians to believe in Jesus' words, pray for the sick, and see amazing results."

—**MARK GISZCZAK**
Augustine Institute, Denver, Colorado

"In a world enchanted with self-made religion, how should the church evangelize? As they did in the early church: by signs to confirm the word. After reviewing the abundant New Testament evidence regarding the strong relationship between preaching and healing, Thelen explores the audience to which the Word is addressed today. Since those touched by growing atheism and the cult of self are more open to tangible events like testimonies of healing than mere proclaimed truths, Thelen challenges preachers and evangelists to pray for signs, especially healings, when they proclaim the Word. Such an approach is not only deeply rooted in scripture, but it is also good advice."

—**GEORGE MONTAGUE**
St. Mary's University, San Antonio, Texas

.

"The New Evangelization will not succeed without a revival of the healing ministry within the Catholic Church. Miraculous healing, as it was for Jesus, is indispensable in proclaiming the gospel for it bears witness to the gospel's saving power. Thelen's small book clearly and lucidly demonstrates the importance of healing in the ministry of Jesus and in the life of the Apostolic Church, and in so doing establishes the importance of the healing ministry in our own day. Thelen's book provides clergy and laity alike the needed theological foundation and the indispensable pastoral inspiration for them to proclaim boldly Jesus' Gospel in the power of the Holy Spirit to the glory of God the Father."

—**THOMAS G. WEINANDY**
Capuchin College, Washington, DC

"Throughout the gospels, Jesus is recognized as one who speaks with authority—his powerful deeds confirm the life-giving message he proclaims. In this short but power-packed book, Thelen proposes that the church must emulate Jesus, so that those within and outside the church may once again experience the power of the Holy Spirit and the divine authority of the gospel message. I encourage every reader to pray unceasingly as you take in the life-changing wisdom contained throughout this book. I strongly believe that its core message will transform the heart of church, as well as the hearts of many lost souls who are seeking God's love and truth."

—BOB SCHUCHTS
John Paul II Healing Center, Tallahassee, Florida

"Mathias Thelen makes a compelling case from the New Testament that signs and wonders and the ministry of healing are essential aspects to the proclamation of the gospel and hold particular promise for evangelization in a post-modern world. His exegesis is particularly astute, weighing judiciously the diverse interpretations of scholars, and noticing implications of texts that most readers miss. This work is well-researched, well-considered, and well-written. The author has a gift for persuasive argument and makes a strong case on an important subject."

—PETER S. WILLIAMSON
Sacred Heart Major Seminary, Archdiocese of Detroit

"People long to be touched by God. They want to know that God sees them and cares about their plight. *Biblical Foundations* provides a solid foundation for the continuation of Jesus mighty works into the modern era. I truly believe that we are entering a period where healing and miraculous signs will cut through the political and social confusion many people face. My hope is that many will realize the refreshing grace of God as they are healed and they will themselves become fruitful disciples in the New Evangelization."

—JEFF CAVINS
Founder of The Great Adventure Bible Study System, Ascension Press

Biblical Foundations for the Role of Healing in Evangelization

Biblical Foundations for the Role of
Healing In Evangelization

Mathias D. Thelen, STL

Foreword by Mary Healy, STD

WIPF & STOCK · Eugene, Oregon

BIBLICAL FOUNDATIONS FOR THE ROLE OF HEALING
IN EVANGELIZATION

Wipf & Stock
An Imprint of Wipf and Stock Publishers
199 W. 8th Ave., Suite 3
Eugene, OR 97401

www.wipfandstock.com

PAPERBACK ISBN: 978-1-5326-3631-8
HARDCOVER ISBN: 978-1-5326-3633-2
EBOOK ISBN: 978-1-5326-3632-5

Manufactured in the U.S.A.   12/07/17

To Patrick and Emily Reis: Your friendship and confidence in the goodness of the God never cease to be a source of inspiration for me.

Contents

Foreword

"BEHOLD, I AM DOING a new thing; now it springs forth, do you not perceive it?" (Isa 43:19). Truly God is doing something new in the church today. As Catholics ardently pursue the call to the new evangelization, God himself is bearing witness to the gospel "by signs and wonders and various miracles and by gifts of the Holy Spirit" (Heb 2:4) on a scale not seen since the early centuries of the church. Yet this "new thing" is in reality a rediscovery of what has always belonged to the inheritance of Christ's followers. The prevalence of healings and miracles in evangelization today is a return to normal.

Fr. Mathias Thelen is among those in the vanguard of the Holy Spirit's new work. I was privileged to direct his thesis for the STL degree (Sacred Theology Licentiate) at Sacred Heart Major Seminary in Detroit, which he developed into this book. Through a close examination of New Testament texts, Fr. Mathias compellingly demonstrates the essential link between healing and evangelization. His work is the fruit of not only competent biblical scholarship, but also of lived experience in putting into practice what Scripture teaches. I have participated in several healing services led by Fr. Mathias in which his preaching of the gospel message was accompanied by numerous healings, both physical and interior, leading many people to deeper faith and some to radical conversion of life.

Fr. Mathias's argument challenges some long-held and often unquestioned assumptions: for instance, that miraculous healings are generally confined to the age of the apostles and the lives of a few great saints, that ordinary people should not expect God to do extraordinary things through them, and that the new evangelization can be carried out effectively without demonstrations of God's power. Those who read it with an open mind may find their paradigm shifting and their vision expanding regarding our access to the power of the Holy Spirit in evangelization.

In sending out his disciples on mission, Jesus asked them to pray that the Lord of the harvest would send out more laborers into his harvest. He also instructed them, "Heal the sick" (Luke 10:2, 9). My hope is that this book will result in many more laborers going out to gather in the harvest, armed with humility and great faith in the Lord's power to heal.

Dr. Mary Healy, STD
Professor of Scripture, Sacred Heart Major Seminary

Acknowledgements

THE LORD HAS SENT so many people into my life who shared with me not only the word of God but their very lives. Without these witnesses to the fidelity of God in Christ, I never would have become a priest and this book would never have been conceived or written. But since there are too many I want to honor and thank, attempting to do so would run the risk of leaving some out.

There are, however, a few men and women I would especially like to thank because without them this particular book would have not been possible. First, I want to thank and honor Fr. William Baer for following the Spirit's lead to introduce to me incredible works of the Spirit in the twentieth century and for taking time to disciple me in the ways of the Spirit. Second, I want to thank my spiritual directors over the years: Fr. John Klockeman, Msgr. Dan Trapp, and Fr. John Horn. SJ, who all clearly identified the work of the Spirit in my life, and as good spiritual fathers, helped me accept the Spirit's work in my life with gratitude so that I would use his gifts in the service of the kingdom. Third, I want to thank several of my seminary professors and now friends, Dr. Ralph Martin, Dr. Peter Williamson, and Dr. Mary Healy, who not only opened my eyes to the riches of biblical and theological scholarship regarding evangelization, but also witnessed to me their deep and contagious love for Jesus and his gospel. Since only those who know and love Jesus deeply want to evangelize, witnessing their ardent passion for evangelization was just as important for me as their academic instruction. Fourth, I want thank Damian Stayne and Dr. Randy Clark for witnessing to me through their lives (and teaching) that there truly is *more* of the Holy Spirit available for the effective proclamation of the word. Their sound teaching and demonstration of how to pray for healing has instilled in me an unbreakable confidence that God wants to manifest his love in the sign of healing much more than most Christians even imagine. Fifth, I would like to thank my friend Ben Pohl for the input and helpful suggestions that made this book possible. Thank you, Ben. Finally, I want to thank my bishop, Earl Boyea, for listening to the Spirit and sending me back to school to complete a License in Sacred Theology through the Pontifical University of St. Thomas Aquinas in Rome.

This short book is a slightly edited version of my S.T.L. thesis, *Biblical Foundations for the Role of Healing in the New Evangelization* (2016) that I wrote under the direction of Dr. Mary Healy. It was truly an honor and a privilege to study the profound truths of Sacred Scripture with such a humble, faith-filled, and competent scholar. May God be praised!

Introduction

THE GREAT DOMINICAN THEOLOGIAN Yves Congar observed in his three-volume work on the Holy Spirit, "Pneumatology, like ecclesiology and theology as a whole, can only develop fully on the basis of what is experienced and realized in the life of the Church. In this sphere, theory is to a great extent dependent on praxis."[1] Theology, in other words, develops in tandem with the experience of the life of the church. Practically, this means that the experience of God in the church has a profound impact on how the church understands what is contained in the sources of revelation, especially sacred Scripture. According to Cardinal Leon Suenens, one of the four moderators of the Second Vatican Council, the experience of God can actually add something to scriptural exegesis, not in the sense that it adds something new but in the sense that it causes the reader to ask new questions.[2] If Congar and Suenens are correct about the relationship between experience and theological development, then the renewal of theology *requires us* not only to be attentive to the lived experience of the church, but also to read the sources of revelation in light of that experience.[3]

1. Congar, *I Believe in the Holy Spirit*, Vol. 1, 172.

2. Suenens, *A New Pentecost*, 99.

3. The theological context of the Congar and Suenens comments above is, in fact, the post-conciliar renewal of theology that was beginning to take into account the church's new experience of the Holy Spirit in 1967 at Duquesne University that rapidly spread throughout the Catholic Church.

Biblical Foundations for the Role of Healing in Evangelization

Among the many things Christians have experienced in the post-conciliar period is the phenomenon of praying for healing and seeing extraordinary results.[4] The sheer number of churches and ecclesial communities (Catholic and Protestant) experiencing physical healing has caused many evangelists and scholars to ask new questions as they study the Scriptures in order to develop a deeper understanding of healing and its place in the Christian life. As a result, passages of Scripture about healing that were thought to be irrelevant to contemporary Christian life (except in their spiritual interpretation) began to come back to life and have been interpreted anew.[5] The rediscovery of the biblical foundations of the ministry of healing, therefore, has followed on the heels of the church's experience of the renewal of the practice of healing prayer itself.

The Catholic Church has been attentive to this phenomenon of healing prayer and has sought to aid in its theological understanding and pastoral care. In 2000, the Congregation for the Doctrine of the Faith (CDF) issued a document entitled "Instruction on Prayers for Healing" that summarizes the scriptural and theological foundations of praying for healing and addresses some pastoral concerns.[6] The next year, the Pontifical Council for the Laity

---

4. Testimonies of such results have become common in some parts of the church. In 2011, Craig Keener published an impressive two-volume study on the credibility of miracles from a biblical, philosophical, and theological perspective. He examines scores of contemporary examples of reports of healing, most of which are commonly happening in Pentecostal/charismatic churches in the global south. See Keener, *Miracles*.

5. The increased phenomena of healing and other gifts of the Holy Spirit in the global church has led some scholars to reiterate the critical importance of reading Scripture from a "Pentecostal hermeneutic" in which the objective meaning of the text about healing and other gifts of the Spirit (word) are interpreted in light of the church's subjective experience of the realities to which text points (Spirit). According to Craig Keener, the authentically Christian hermeneutic of Scripture is a reading of Scripture in light of Pentecost that "invites all Christians into the biblical world, summoning us to expectancy and trust in God's present, often surprising working in his church and in our lives." Keener, *Spirit Hermeneutics*, 287.

6. Congregation for the Doctrine for the Faith, "Instruction on Prayers for Healing," n.p.

and the International Catholic Charismatic Renewal Services (IC-CRS) sponsored a colloquium on the subject of healing prayer to discuss this document. Participants included theologians, evangelists, and pastors from all over the world who took care to discuss topics ranging from deep theological reflections on Scripture to the pastoral concerns and issues regarding healing ministry in the Catholic Church.[7] In 2007, the Doctrinal Commission of ICCRS published the important document *Guidelines on Prayers for Healing* which was intended as a pastoral application of the 2000 CDF document.[8] The commission writes, "While in recent years there has been a worldwide effort to energize the Church for a 'new evangelization,' following the call of Pope John Paul II, relatively little attention has been given to the place of the ministry of healing in the proclamation of the gospel."[9] This short book represents one modest attempt to address this concern.

In the context of the lived experience of the church in which the practice of healing prayer and physical healings are becoming more common, the scriptural question of how healing is related to evangelization becomes all the more important. It is undeniable that the various healings in the New Testament—both in the ministry of Jesus and that of the disciples—play a significant role in bringing people to faith. But what exactly is the relationship between healing and the preaching of the gospel in Scripture? Are we to understand the healings of the New Testament as unique phenomena limited to Jesus and the disciples and, therefore, extraordinarily rare today? Or are healings so essential to the proclamation of the gospel that they constitute an almost inseparable aspect of that proclamation? Given the serious challenges facing the church in the postmodern world, especially in the West where millions of Christians no longer practice the faith, the answer to these biblical questions has critical implications for how the church effectively proclaims the gospel of Jesus Christ.

---

7. The proceedings of this colloquium are found in the volume, ICCRS and Pontifical Council for the Laity, *Prayer for Healing: International Colloquium.*

8. Doctrinal Commission of ICCRS, *Guidelines on Prayers for Healing.*

9. Ibid., 42.

This book examines the role that physical healing plays in the proclamation of the gospel in the New Testament and applies these insights to the new evangelization. It does not treat in an exhaustive, or even in a summary, way the healings in the New Testament. Instead, various passages on healings will be addressed and examined in order to draw out the precise role they have in the proclamation of that gospel. While the purpose of healings will be discussed in their *evangelistic* value, such as leading to repentance and faith, a full theology of healing in which the diverse theological aspects of healing in Scripture are discussed is beyond the scope of this book. Thus, passages regarding the practice of healing prayer not related to the preaching of the gospel, such as James's injunction to call for the presbyters to pray for the sick (Jas 5:13-18), will not be considered.

The flow of the book is fairly straightforward. Chapter 1 examines healing in the ministry of Jesus as it relates to the preaching of the gospel. Many aspects of Jesus' healing ministry are considered: healing and the kingdom, healing and the power of testimony, healing as signs given for the purpose of eliciting faith, and the transference of Jesus' ministry to his disciples in the various commissioning accounts where the connection between preaching and healing is especially clear. Chapter 2 examines the Acts of the Apostles as the continuation of the ministry of Jesus in the early church, who receives at Pentecost the same anointing that Jesus received at his baptism. Sharing in Jesus' anointing, the church does what Jesus did and healing plays a significant role in their preaching of the gospel in Acts. In chapter 3 we examine the Pauline corpus to discover the ways in which Paul discusses the gospel that comes in the power of the Spirit and its effect on his hearers in terms of healing. We will also examine the meaning of the charism of healing in Paul's letters and discuss how seeking the higher gifts is related to evangelization. In the concluding chapter, we will discuss how healing is uniquely positioned to meet the challenge of engaging the postmodern world of today with the gospel. Then, based on the research of the book, we will offer some biblical, theological, and pastoral orientations for the church as it moves forward in integrating the Spirit-given power for healing into the proclamation of the gospel. The result is a clarion call for an increase of faith in God who pours out his Spirit to give the church boldness in proclaiming Jesus with power as he confirms the message of the gospel through signs, wonders, and healings.

Chapter 1

Healing and Evangelization
in the Ministry of Jesus

THIS CHAPTER ATTEMPTS TO define more precisely the role physical healings play in Jesus' and the disciples' preaching of the gospel. We will first examine the relationship between Jesus' preaching of the kingdom of God and healing by considering the nature of the kingdom of God. Then we will consider the role testimony of healing plays in bringing people to faith in Jesus. This leads to our consideration of the healings of Jesus as signs meant to elicit faith in him as the Messiah and the Son of God. Finally, we will examine the relationship between healing and the commissioning of the disciples to preach the gospel. After examining the ministry of Jesus in this way, we will synthesize the relationship between healing and evangelization in the Gospels.

Healing and the Proclamation of the Kingdom

After John's arrest, Jesus enters into Galilee preaching the gospel of God: "The time is fulfilled, and the kingdom of God is at hand; repent, and believe in the gospel" (Mark 1:15, RSVCE). The proclamation of the good news of the kingdom is why Jesus came: "I must preach the good news of the kingdom of God to the other cities, for I was sent for this purpose" (Luke 4:43). The kingdom of God is not simply a message of good news about God's reign; it is the making present of that reign in and through the ministry and person of Jesus.[1] The inbreaking of the kingdom of God through the ministry of Jesus and the need to enter it through a personal response of repentance and faith is at the heart of Jesus' earthly ministry. In order for us to understand the relationship between the message about God's reign in Jesus and the deeds of Jesus (i.e., healing), we need to briefly examine the *manner* in which the kingdom of God is made present in Jesus' ministry. In other words, we need to understand how the kingdom of God is "at hand."

Jesus first preaches the kingdom in the "time of fulfillment." According to Mary Healy, "the time of fulfillment means that now, in Jesus, God is breaking into history to fulfill his promises and bring his whole plan to completion. It is a decisive moment, a turning point."[2] God is acting in history to set his people free in and through his reign which is mysteriously present in Jesus. According to George Eldon Ladd, the mystery of the kingdom is presented in three stages in the New Testament: (1) There are passages that present the kingdom of God as God's reign, his rule; (2) other passages describe the kingdom as God's reign that has broken into time and in which people can experience its blessings in the present; and finally, (3) other passages speak about a future realm in which people will experience the fullness of his reign.[3] In putting these three stages together with the biblical texts, Ladd concludes that in Jesus the future realm (heaven) has broken into time and, therefore, the blessings associated with God's full rule and reign in heaven are manifested in the ministry of Jesus on Earth.[4] In other words, the kingdom of God as proclaimed and

1. Healy, *Gospel of Mark*, 41.

2. Ibid., 41.

3. Ladd, *The Gospel of the Kingdom*, 22.

4. Ibid., 23. Ladd also maintains that, "If God's kingdom is a gift of life bestowed upon his people when he manifests his rule in eschatological glory, and if God's kingdom is also God's rule invading history before the eschatological consummation, it follows that we may expect God's rule in the present to bring a preliminary blessing to his people." Ladd, *A Theology of the New*

manifested in Jesus represents an "already but not yet" eschatology in which the kingdom and its blessings are present in a *provisional* way, for it will not be complete until the future consummation of the kingdom in heaven.[5] Since the blessings of the future kingdom of God are made present in Jesus' ministry, the preaching of that kingdom marks the beginning of the definitive destruction of the works of the devil.[6]

The Gospels often depict sickness or illness as works of the devil, at least indirectly if not directly.[7] While in the Gospel of Mark there is often a clear distinction between healing and deliverance, the lines are blurred in Matthew and Luke to such an extent that one can argue that the evangelists believed that illness is generally caused by Satan or demons. In fact, deliverance from the influence of evil spirits often results in people's physical healings.[8] While we need not conclude that all sickness has demonic origins, we can understand the healings of Jesus as the beginning of the breaking of the devil's hold on the world.[9] David Stanley writes:

Testament, 70.

5. Ladd's eschatology, also known as "inaugurated eschatology," is at the foundation of healing evangelist John Wimber's theology of the kingdom. Randy Clark and many other healing evangelists take Ladd's view of the Kingdom as a theological foundation from which they understand the healings of Jesus and the possibility of healing happening today. For an evangelical evaluation of Ladd's eschatology, see Moore, *The Kingdom of Christ,* 30–48. For Ladd's succinct overview on this topic, see Ladd, *The Presence of the Future,* 149–218.

6. In describing the kingdom of God in Luke, Scripture scholar Frank Matera puts it this way: "Jesus' healings and exorcisms are concrete indications of the inbreaking kingdom of God that is already present in Jesus' ministry. They are examples of how salvation affects people here and now by freeing them from sin and sickness, the oppression of evil spirits, and restoring them to the human community . . . The salvation Jesus proclaims during his earthly ministry is a present reality that already affects people 'today' (4:21; 19:9; 23:43). It restores them to health and releases them from Satan's bondage; it offers forgiveness and effects a reversal of fortunes." Matera, *New Testament Theology,* 70–71.

7. Turner, "Holy Spirit," 346.

8. Bell, "Demon, Devil, Satan," 196; and Hendrickx, *The Miracle Stories of the Synoptic Gospels,* 11–12.

9. If death came into the world through sin (Rom 5:12), then bodily

For Mark, the cures wrought by Jesus constitute the initial frontal attack upon the "kingdom" of Satan. Jesus has
come to inaugurate the establishment of the kingdom of
God in history; and he must begin by breaking the hold
of evil upon the world, liberating men from the thrall of
the "strong man," Satan.[10]

That Jesus understands sickness as something that Satan can
use to bind people is evident also in his words in the story of the
healing of the crippled woman on the Sabbath: "And ought not this
woman, a daughter of Abraham whom Satan bound for eighteen
years, be loosed from this bond on the Sabbath day?" (Luke 13:16).
Jesus' healing of this woman is understood as the destruction of a
work of the devil. Seeing that some sickness is the direct work of
the devil leads John Wimber to describe Jesus as a "divine invader"
who begins to take back territory from the devil. "When Jesus said
that the kingdom of God had come in him, he claimed for himself
the position of a divine invader, coming to set everything straight,
'The reason why the Son of God appeared was to destroy the works
of the devil.'"[11]

Given the understanding of the "already but not yet" nature
of the kingdom of God, we are now in a position to situate more
precisely the healings that accompanied Jesus' proclamation with
the proclamation itself. In proclaiming the gospel, Jesus begins to
destroy the power of the kingdom of darkness by which man is
enslaved to the devil. Ladd explains:

"God is now acting among men to deliver them from
bondage to Satan. It is the announcement that God, in
the person of Christ, is doing something—if you please,
is attacking the very kingdom of Satan himself. The

---

sickness which leads to death can be understood as indirectly related to the
time when sin entered the world through the original sin of Adam, which happened as the result of the devil's temptation. So at least generally, sickness can
be seen as a result of sin which was provoked by the devil.

10. Stanley, "Salvation and Healing," 301. Stanley also understands this to
be true for Matthew and Luke as well. as discussed on pages 311 and 313.

11. Wimber and Springer, *Power Evangelism*, 30.

> exorcism of demons is proof that the kingdom of God
> has come among men and is at work among them."[12]

If sickness, disease, and death are works of Satan, then the presence of the kingdom of God, even in a provisional way, would see the destruction of these works. Randy Clark puts it this way: "One of the ways Jesus destroyed the works of the devil was to minister healing and deliverance to the sick and afflicted."[13]

If Jesus destroys the kingdom of darkness through healing and deliverance, then it is no surprise that as Jesus proclaims that the kingdom of God is *at hand*, his proclamation is accompanied by the *demonstration* of the presence and power of that kingdom through signs of healing and deliverance from evil spirits. Such proclamation and demonstration by Jesus marks the *beginning* of God transferring his people from the "dominion of darkness" into the kingdom of his beloved Son (Col 1:13).[14] It is quite significant then that Peter in the Acts of the Apostles understands Jesus' healings and deliverances as acts which free people from the oppression of the devil: "God anointed Jesus of Nazareth with the Holy Spirit and with power; how he went about doing good and healing all that were oppressed by the devil, for God was with him" (Acts 10:38).

An important illustration of the power of the inbreaking kingdom of God is the healing of the blind demoniac in Matthew 12:22–32.[15] The Pharisees, in their unbelief, are attempting to explain that Jesus' power to heal comes from Satan. After Jesus shows

---

12. Ladd, *The Gospel of the Kingdom,* 47. On this point Pope Benedict XVI agrees: "The authority to cast out demons and to free the world from their dark threat, for the sake of the one true God, is the same authority that rules out any magical understanding of healing through attempts to manipulate these mysterious powers . . . God's dominion, God's kingdom, means precisely the disempowerment of these forces by the intervention of the one God, who is good, who is the Good itself." Pope Benedict XVI, *Jesus of Nazareth,* 176.

13. Clark, *Power to Heal,* 25.

14. The beginning of this transference begins definitively in the paschal mystery of Christ's death, resurrection, ascension, and the subsequent outpouring of the Holy Spirit.

15. See also Luke 11:14–22.

the foolishness of this response by stating that a kingdom divided against itself cannot stand, he drives the point home: "And if I cast out demons by Beelzebul, by whom do your sons cast them out? Therefore they shall be your judges. But if it is by the Spirit of God that I cast out demons, then the kingdom of God has come upon you" (Matt 12:28). What the Pharisees are identifying as Satan is, in fact, the Spirit of God whose activity through Jesus is a dramatic sign of the inbreaking of God's kingdom in which man is healed and set free from the power of Satan's kingdom.[16] The proclamation of the kingdom in Jesus' ministry is, therefore, demonstrated through the destruction of the devil's works by the power of the Spirit.

Understanding the proclamation of the inbreaking kingdom of God in terms of destroying the works of the devil helps us understand why Jesus heals as he preaches the gospel of the kingdom:

> And he went about all Galilee, teaching in their synagogues and preaching the gospel of the kingdom and healing every disease and every infirmity among the people. So his fame spread throughout all Syria, and they brought to him all the sick, those afflicted with various disease and pains, demoniacs, epileptics, and paralytics, and he healed them. And great crowds followed him. (Matt 4:23–25)

Again, in chapter 9:

> And Jesus went about all the cities and villages, teaching in their synagogues and preaching the gospel of the kingdom, and healing every disease and every infirmity. When he saw the crowds, he had compassion for them, because they were harassed and helpless, like sheep without a shepherd. (Matt 9:35)

The Lukan parallel also shows the universality of Jesus' healing:

> And he came down with them and stood on a level place, with a great crowd of his disciples and a great multitude of people from all Judea and Jerusalem and the seacoast

16. Sri and Mitch, *The Gospel of Matthew*, 168–69.

of Tyre and Sidon, who came to hear him and to be healed of their diseases, and those who were troubled with unclean spirits were cured. And all the crowd sought to touch him, for power came forth from him and healed them all. (Luke 6:17–19)

Further, when Jesus leaves the house of Peter's mother-in-law, he heals everyone who comes to him: "Now when the sun was setting, all those who had any that were sick with various diseases brought them to him; and he laid his hands on every one of them and healed them" (Luke 4:40).

In light of Jesus' prolific healing ministry, it is important to note that Jesus did not have the goal of healing everyone, nor did he accomplish such a thing. It is false to conclude that because Jesus heals every person in the passages above that the fullness of the kingdom of God in which everyone is healed can be expected here on Earth. Such an expectation represents a misapplication of the "already but not yet" nature of the inbreaking presence of the kingdom. Even in the earthly ministry of Jesus, the presence of the kingdom on Earth is partial and provisional; all the people Jesus heals are still subject to further sickness and death. Therefore, because the inbreaking kingdom of God is an "already but not yet" reality, healings will always be provisional gifts of God in response to faith but never automatic or complete.[17]

Nevertheless, the deeds of healing and deliverance performed in the context of Jesus' preaching serve as signs of the presence of the very kingdom that is preached. Here we can discern the *intrinsic link* between the proclamation of the Gospel and the healing ministry of Jesus; as the kingdom of God is preached, signs of the

17. For an important discussion on the provisional nature of healing see Francis Sullivan, *Charisms and Charismatic Renewal*, 163–69. See also Max Turner, *The Holy Spirit and Spiritual Gifts in the New Testament Church and Today*, 250–54 and 330–35. Derek Morphew, in his study on the kingdom of God, argues that those who teach a theology in which everyone will be healed if enough faith is present have essentially confused the "already" with the "not yet" and have missed the understanding of redemption. Because the presence of the kingdom is provisional in this world, healing will always be selective and provisional. Morphew, *Breakthrough*, 183–87.

presence of the kingdom, including healing, are made manifest. Randy Clark puts it this way: "In advancing the kingdom of God, Jesus healed, cast out demons, prophesied, and ministered in other supernatural ways. This was the message of the kingdom—the good news that the kingdom of God had dawned and broken out among mankind."[18] If this is true, there cannot be a real separation between the proclamation and the demonstration of that proclamation.

It is difficult to avoid the conclusion that since the healings of Jesus are concrete signs that make present the inbreaking of God's kingdom they form part of the very message of the kingdom. Miracles and healings are the "gospel in action."[19] As the gospel in action, they *express* the presence of the kingdom and, therefore, cannot be reduced to signs external to the gospel itself. In this way, the healings of Jesus are intrinsic to the gospel.[20] Cardinal Albert Vanhoye maintains that the "healings [of Jesus] were not only a manifestation of power, they were also, and above all, an expression of merciful loving-kindness, and for that reason they have an even more intimate linkage with the kingdom of God."[21]

The miracles that accompany preaching the message of the kingdom also have a significant role in leading people to a personal response of faith in the gospel.

> For the duration of his public ministry, Jesus demonstrated that the kingdom of God was near by healing the sick, casting out demons, and raising the dead. Every miraculous act had a purpose: to confront people with

18. Clark, *The Essential Guide to the Power of the Holy Spirit*, 126.

19. According to Randy Clark, "Instead of being limited to simply proving doctrine, the miracles were part of the good news, signaling the inbreaking of the kingdom of God. Miracles do not just confirm or prove the gospel: they are the gospel in action." Clark, *Essential Guide to the Power*, 108.

20. Max Turner suggests the healings of Jesus do not simply serve to legitimize his message. But as *concrete expressions* of Jesus' message, healings are a part of the message itself. Turner, *The Holy Spirit and Spiritual Gifts*, 243. Francis MacNutt makes a similar point in *Healing*, 75.

21. VanHoye, "Healings in the Life of Jesus and in the Early Church," 35.

his message that in him the kingdom of God had come
and that they had to decide to accept or reject it.[22]

When people encounter the gospel of the kingdom where
God's love for man is manifested in deeds of healing and deliverance, they can see more clearly the truth of the kingdom of God
to which they are invited. According to the Doctrinal Commission of ICCRS, "Every healing is to be understood as a sign of
the once-and-for-all victory of Jesus in his cross and resurrection, made present here and now as a pledge of complete healing and eternal glory in the coming kingdom."[23] Therefore, those
who encounter the "already but not yet" nature of the kingdom
through its message and demonstration of healings are drawn by
the merciful compassion of God, who offers them—through the
forgiveness of sins—the *fullness of salvation* to live with him in the
kingdom of heaven. Understanding the full scope of redemption
in and through the signs of the kingdom allows one to make a
decision for or against it. The gospel of the kingdom that comes
in both word and deed enables people to understand the nature of
the kingdom of God to which they are invited, thereby confronting
them with a choice to accept or reject the invitation to enter into
that kingdom (Matt 22:1–14).

Healing and the Power of Testimony

Jesus' healings are arguably the chief reason people are initially
attracted to him in the New Testament. As Jesus proclaims the
kingdom of God, he draws great crowds precisely because of his
healings and miracles. This is evident in the Gospel of John where

22. Wimber, *Power Evangelism*, 27.

23. Doctrinal Commission of the ICCRS, *Guidelines on Prayers*, 37. That
Jesus understands sin as the ultimate sickness that he intends to heal is evident
in Mark 2:17, "Those who are well have no need of a physician, but those who
are sick; I have come to call not the righteous but sinners." In this way, the
physical healings of Jesus are not only concrete manifestations of the kingdom
on Earth but they are signs that point to the final healing of the whole person
in the eternal kingdom of heaven.

"a multitude followed [Jesus], because they saw the signs which he did on those who were diseased" (John 6:2). It is often in the context of healing that Jesus preaches the kingdom and invites his listeners to faith so as to enter the kingdom. That Jesus' healing causes many to follow him and hear his preaching is clear in Matthew 4:23–25:

> And he went about all Galilee, teaching in their synagogues and preaching the gospel of the kingdom and healing every disease and every infirmity among the people. So his *fame* spread through all Syria, and they brought him all the sick, those afflicted with various diseases and pains, demoniacs, epileptics, and paralytics, and he healed them. And *great crowds* followed him from Galilee and from the Decapolis and Jerusalem and Judea and from beyond the Jordan. (emphasis mine)

The connection between Jesus' fame and his healing every disease is clear in this passage. The reason why "they brought him all the sick" was that Jesus became famous by "healing every disease and every infirmity among the people." The healing that accompanied his preaching had the effect of attracting great crowds. It is critical, therefore, to note that it is precisely in this context of drawing great crowds through healing that Jesus in the next verse begins to preach the Sermon on the Mount. "Seeing the crowds, he went up on the mountain, and when he sat down his disciples came to him. And he opened his mouth and taught them . . ." (Matt 4:25–5:1).[24] The crowds who were attracted to Jesus on account of his healings are able to hear the message of the kingdom of God in the Sermon on the Mount. The parallel passage in Luke makes the connection between the message of the gospel and healing even clearer: "A great multitude of people . . . *came to hear him and to be healed* of their diseases; those who were troubled with unclean spirits were cured. And all the crowd sought to touch him, for power came forth from him and healed them all" (Luke 6:17–19,

---

24. The context of the Sermon on the Mount in Matthew's gospel indicates that the audience was not simply the inner band of the disciples, but "the crowds" (Matt 7:28).

emphasis mine). The multitudes came for two reasons: to hear Jesus speak and to be healed.

From these passages, we can conclude that the signs of healings that Jesus worked played a significant role in bringing the multitudes to him. That people were initially drawn to Jesus does not entail that they became full disciples by a personal response to Jesus in faith and repentance.[25] Rather, the point here is simply to note that Jesus' healings played a significant role in attracting and drawing people to him so they could hear the gospel and have an *opportunity* to respond to Jesus in faith and enter the kingdom that was preached.[26]

We also find in the Gospels both those who experienced healing and those who witnessed healings spreading the word about Jesus. After Jesus tells the man who was healed of leprosy not to tell anyone about his healing, the text says: "But so much the more the report went abroad concerning him; and great multitudes gathered to hear and to be healed of their infirmities" (Luke 5:15). The report of his healing led to more people wanting to come to Jesus. In the Gospel of Matthew, there seems to be evidence of the testimony of a particular healing leading others to approach Jesus in faith for healing. In Matthew 9, the woman healed of a hemorrhage of twelve years said to herself prior to her healing, "If I only touch his garment, I shall be made well" (9:21). It is interesting that this precise line of thinking is present among those who later came to Jesus in Matthew 14: "And when the men of that place recognized him, they sent round to all that region and brought to him all that were sick, and they begged him that they might only touch the fringe of his garment and as many as touched it were made well" (Matt 14:35–36). How did they know that touching his garment could bring healing? A strong argument can be made that the testimony of the healed woman must have been widespread.[27]

---

25. For example, later in John 6 even disciples turn away from Jesus because of the "hard saying" of eating his body and drinking his blood.

26. One's personal response to Jesus is what determines his entry into the kingdom (Mark 4:10–20, Matt 13:9, and Luke 8:4–15).

27. Clark, "Prayer for Healing," n.p.

We cannot doubt that as people were healed by Jesus and shared their testimony, others came to him precisely because of the signs of healing he was performing. Healing, therefore, plays an irreplaceable role in attracting people to Jesus who in turn hear his preaching, which opens them up to repentance and faith.

Healing as a Sign that Elicits Faith

In examining the role healing plays in coming to faith in Jesus, it is necessary to grasp how Jesus himself understands his messianic mission which includes healing. Understanding Jesus' actions in light of his messianic mission helps us to more precisely see the place healing has in his mission to proclaim the good news. The scope of Jesus' mission is outlined in Luke 4 when Jesus reads from Isaiah 61 in the synagogue at Nazareth:

> He opened the book and found the place where it is written, "The Spirit of the Lord is upon me because he has anointed me to preach good news to the poor. He has sent me to proclaim release to captives and recovering of sight to the blind, to set at liberty those who are oppressed, to proclaim the acceptable year of the Lord." And he closed the book, and gave it back to the attendant, and sat down; and the eyes of all in the synagogue were fixed on him. And he began to say to them, "Today this Scripture has been fulfilled in your hearing" (Luke 4:17–21).

In his declaration that Isaiah 61:1–2 is fulfilled in their hearing, Jesus boldly claims to those present that he is the Messiah, the one anointed by the Spirit of God for the purpose of preaching the good news (εὐαγγελίσασθαι) to the poor.[28] This prophetic anointing for preaching, or evangelization as the Greek word suggests, also involves the mission to *release captives* and the *recovering of*

---

28. According to George Montague, the Spirit of the Lord upon Jesus in the Gospel of Luke replaces the theme of the inbreaking coming of the Kingdom we see in Mark and Matthew. Already in the synoptic tradition, there is a close relationship between the anointing of the Spirit and the coming of the kingdom. Montague, *The Holy Spirit*, 264.

sight to the blind.[29] The proclamation of the good news and deeds of healing are thus united in Jesus' messianic mission in the Spirit. Bertold Klappert writes:

> The healings are part of Jesus' word and are not to be detached from his proclamation. According to Lk 4:18, Jesus related the prophetic word of Isa. 62:1f to his own mission. God sent him to bring good news to the poor and sight to the blind. This denotes the unity of word and deed in Jesus' proclamation . . . the proclamation of the kingdom of God takes place by means of Jesus' word, and Jesus' healings are the physical expression of his word.[30]

The one prophetic mission of the Messiah, therefore, has two aspects: words and deeds.[31] Since they form a unity in Jesus' mission, the former imply the latter and the latter require the former. Like the word of the prophet, the word of Jesus, therefore, has a special character in that one cannot separate the content of his preaching from the powerful effect of his deeds.[32] This inextricable

29. There are other Old Testament passages which prophesy the time of the Messiah being a time of healing. One clear example is Isaiah 35:3–6: "Strengthen the weak hands, and make firm the feeble knees. Say to those who are of a fearful heart, 'Be strong, fear not! Behold, your God will come with vengeance, with the recompense of God. He will come and save you.' Then the eyes of the blind shall be opened, and the ears of the deaf unstopped then shall the lame man leap like a hart, and the tongue of the dumb sing for joy. For waters shall break forth in the wilderness, and streams in the desert."

30. Klappert, "λόγος," 1108.

31. In his doctoral dissertation, Leo O'Reilly argues that there is an essential unity of word and deed in Jesus' ministry. "At his baptism, Jesus was anointed as prophet; he was called by God and entrusted with the mission of announcing the good news of eschatological salvation in word and deed . . . [This unity of word and deed] is best illustrated by the words of the disciples on the road to Emmaus who described him as a prophet, mighty in deed and word. A look at the Gospels shows how Luke is at pains to link both aspects of Jesus' ministry, his preaching and his miracles, right back to his baptismal anointing with the Spirit. This in turn enables him to integrate both of these activities into a unified ministry of the word." O' Reilly, *Word and Sign in the Acts of the Apostles*, 32.

32. Jesus' word, according to O'Reilly, is like that of the Old Testament prophet; it has both a *dianoetic* aspect (message) and a *dynamic* aspect (power).

unity of word and deed is exactly what Luke shows in Jesus' Spirit-filled ministry.

The deeds of the Messiah are also the signs that Jesus uses to authenticate his messianic identity when John the Baptist sends his own disciples to inquire about Jesus.

> John the Baptist has sent us to you, saying, 'Are you he who is to come or shall we look for another?' In that hour he cured many of the diseases and plagues and evil spirits, and on many that were blind he bestowed sight. And he answered them, 'Go and tell John what you have seen and heard: the blind received their sign, the lame walk, lepers are cleansed, and the deaf hear, the dead are raised up, the poor have good news preached to them. Blessed is he who takes no offense at me. (Luke 9:18–24)

If the healings of Jesus here serve as *signs* that authenticate his identity as the Messiah, then they are not accidental to his ministry but are essential to it; they signify and point to the fact that he is the long-awaited Messiah who will come to redeem Israel. If the deeds of healing are signs that Jesus is the Spirit-anointed Messiah, then their presence among the disciples will also serve as signs that Jesus is present with them by means of his Spirit.[33]

In Matthew 11, Jesus' strong rebuke against the unbelief of the people of Chorazin and Bethsaida in the face of his mighty deeds, which include healing, reveals that these deeds are given to evoke a personal response of repentance and faith.

> Then he began to upbraid the cities where most of his mighty works had been done, because they did not repent. 'Woe to you, Chorazin! Woe to you, Bethsaida! For

---

Thus, Jesus' word has both intelligible content and the power to effect change. The intelligible content of Jesus' word can be characterized as the message of salvation, whereas the deeds that Jesus performs such as healings and miracles constitute the powerful *effect* of the word of salvation he preaches. O'Reilly explains, "Jesus' deeds of power are word-events. His words are not merely words of teaching. They are also active, healing words in the 'power' of the Spirit and his 'preaching the good news' is proclamation in word and action." Ibid., 39–40.

33. This point is discussed in more detail in the next chapter.

> if the mighty works done in you had been done in Tyre
> and Sidon, they would have repented long ago in sack-
> cloth and ashes . . . For if the mighty works done in you
> had been done in Sodom, it would have remained until
> this day. (Matt 11:20–21, 23–24)

The failure to repent in the presence of his mighty deeds exposes the unbelief of these towns and, therefore, provokes Jesus to pronounce a judgment more severe than the one given to the wicked Gentile cities of Tyre, Sidon, and Sodom in the Old Testament.[34] There is something about the failure to repent and believe in the midst of Jesus' mighty works that elicits judgment. The harsh judgment of these unbelieving cities leads Gary Greig to conclude that the refusal to believe in the midst of Jesus' signs leads to judgment *because* Jesus' miraculous works and healings are intended to produce repentance and faith in him.[35] Only in this way does the harsh judgment Jesus pronounces upon Chorazin and Bethsaida make sense. Put another way, it is precisely because Jesus' mighty deeds and healings are done for the purpose of eliciting repentance and faith that the refusal to believe in them invokes judgment. From this passage we can conclude the mighty deeds and healings of Jesus either lead people to faith in him, or expose their hidden unbelief and rejection of him.[36]

The Gospel of John gives us a more profound interplay between faith and unbelief in Jesus in light of the signs that he performs.[37] One of the more striking examples of a healing that

---

34. Sri, *The Gospel of Matthew*, 157–58.

35. Greig, *The Kingdom and the Power*, 147.

36. In manifesting the reality of the kingdom to the senses in an undeniable way, the healings of Jesus seem to remove any possible "middle ground" in one's stance toward him. Those who have witnessed his healings cannot remain neutral. Healings, therefore, have the power to force people who witness or experience them into a point of decision regarding whether or not to believe in Jesus. See Johnson, *When Heaven Invades Earth*, 120–21.

37. According to C. Wahlen, the signs (or miracles) in John's Gospel are given to progressively lead the characters in the story of the gospel (and the reader) "to the unique identity of Jesus as the Son and his intimate knowledge of and obedience to the Father." Wahlen, "Healing," 363.

serves as a sign meant to elicit faith in Jesus is that of the man born blind in John 9:1–41. The story begins with the disciples asking Jesus whose sin caused the man's blindness. Jesus indicates that the man's sickness is meant to reveal God's works: "It was not that this man sinned, or his parents, but that the works of God might be made manifest in him" (John 9:4). After the man is healed, the rest of the story revolves around the identity of this Jesus who healed him. The unbelieving Pharisees cannot admit that Jesus healed him because Jesus is considered a sinner who does not keep the Sabbath; thus, they also cannot admit that Jesus is from God. After the Pharisees deny that Jesus is from God, the healed man unveils the logic of their unbelief: "Why this is a marvel! You do not know where he comes from, and yet he opened my eyes . . . If this man were not from God, he could do nothing" (John 9:30).

The implication here is that only someone from God could do such a sign. The sign of healing is meant to point to Jesus' identity as one coming from God, and this is precisely what John is showing the reader. It is important that Jesus then elicits faith from the blind man: "'Do you believe in the Son of Man?' He answers, 'And who is he, sir that I may believe in him?' Jesus said to him, 'You have seen him, and it is he who speaks to you.' He said, 'Lord, I believe'; and he worshiped him" (John 9:35–38). The healing of the blind man serves as a sign that opens the blind man up to Jesus' divine identity, and therefore to faith. Once Jesus reveals himself, the healed man is able to respond in faith to Jesus.[38]

In chapter 10, the Jews ask Jesus directly: "'If you are the Christ, tell us plainly.' Jesus answered them, 'I told you and you do not believe. The works that I do in my Father's name, they bear witness to me; but you do not believe, because you do not belong to my sheep'" (John 10:25). Because the Jews do not believe Jesus' words, Jesus points directly to his *works*—the most recent being the healing he performed in chapter 9—because they bear witness to his identity.[39] One cannot separate Jesus' identity from his

---

38. Keener, *Gospel of John*, 795.

39. "Works" (ἔργα) in the Gospel of John refer to miraculous deeds including healing in many places 5:20, 36; 7:3; 9:3–4; 10:25, 32–33, 37–38; 15:24. See

works. Jesus makes the connection between his works and faith just a few verses later:

> If I am not doing the works of my Father, then do not believe me; but if I do them, even though you do not believe me, believe the works, that you may know and understand that the Father is in me and I am in the Father. (John 10:37–39)

The works that Jesus performs are so fundamental to believing in him that Jesus implies that if he is not doing them, they should *not* believe. Francis Martin and William Wright explain this verse this way:

> Jesus' opponents refuse to believe his words, but they are somewhat disposed to his works, which they seem to acknowledge as 'good' (10:32). He encourages them to believe the works, which bear witness to him (10:25). If viewed properly, they are a means by which people can come to believe in him. By coming to faith in this way, Jesus says, you may realize and understand that the Father is in me and I am in the Father.[40]

Because the works of Jesus point to where he is from (the Father) they perform the function of leading people to faith in Jesus. Again, Jesus says even more clearly that his works are reasons for believing in him:

> Do you not believe that I am in the Father and the Father is in me? The words that I say to you I do not speak on my own authority; but the Father who dwells in me does his works. Believe me that I am in the Father and the Father is in me; or else believe me for the sake of the works themselves. (John 14:10–11)

From these passages, we can conclude that Jesus' works of healing are signs meant to elicit faith in him as the Messiah and

---

Keener, *The Gospel of John*, 946. Raymond Brown also understands "works" in John's Gospel as Jesus' designation of miracles. See Brown, *The Gospel According to John 1-12*, 224.

40. Martin and Wright, *The Gospel of John*, 199.

the Son of God.⁴¹ But like in the Synoptic Gospels, these signs also unmask and reveal the unbelief of those who refuse to repent and believe in Jesus.⁴²

Healing and the Mission of the Disciples

One of the clearest ways to understand the role of healing in the preaching of the gospel is to look at the commissioning accounts of Jesus' disciples. The Gospel of John's short commissioning account is packed with implications for the place of healing in in the preaching of the gospel. The risen Jesus appears in the midst of the disciples in the upper room: "Jesus said to them again, 'Peace be with you. As the Father has sent me, even so I send you.' And when he had said this, he breathed on them" (John 20:21–22). Jesus gives his Spirit to the disciples so that they can continue the mission that he received from the Father. According to Craig Keener, the mission of the disciples is not limited to preaching about Jesus in words, but also includes performing works like Jesus did.

> Because Jesus was sending "just as" (καθὼς) the Father sent him (20:21) the disciples would carry on Jesus' mission, including not only signs pointing to Jesus (14:12)

41. Perhaps the clearest evidence that John understood the signs of Jesus in terms of eliciting faith in Jesus is John 20:30–31: "Now Jesus did many other signs in the presence of the disciples, which are not written in this book; but these are written that you may believe that Jesus is the Christ, the Son of God, and that by believing you may have life in his name."

42. There are many other passages that show the connection between Jesus' healing and faith in him. An especially clear example is found in Matthew 9 (cf. Mark 2), where Jesus demonstrates his authority to forgive sin through the healing of the paralytic. This healing is meant to elicit faith in him so that the deeper healing that Jesus has come to bring, the forgiveness of sins, can be obtained. As the Doctrinal Commission of ICCRS says, "Just as physical ailments are symbolic of the various forms of spiritual infirmity that afflict fallen humanity, such as spiritual blindness, deafness, or paralysis, so physical healing is an outward sign of the interior restoration that occurs through the forgiveness of sins." See Doctrinal Commission of the ICCRS, *Guidelines on Prayers*, 31.

but also witness (15:27) through which the Spirit would continue Jesus' presence and work (16:7–11).[43]

Keener points to John 14:12 as evidence that signs, or works, are part of the mission of the disciples: "Truly, truly, I say to you, he who believes in me will also do the works that I do; and greater works than these will he do, because I go to the Father." These "works" include signs of healing that lead people to faith in him. Commenting on this passage, Keener writes,

> The disciples should do miraculous works through faith (though such signs by themselves cannot produce faith and must be supplemented with proclamation which remains central, cf. 20:29) as well as continue Jesus' ministry in other respects . . . The promise of "greater works" calls John's audience to look not only backward but also to the present, where Christ continues to remain active through his presence by the Paraclete and his proclaimed word.[44]

In breathing on his disciples in John 20:22, Jesus gives the disciples his Spirit, empowering them to bear witness to him and do the works he did and even greater ones. The disciples are empowered with Jesus' own Spirit and are sent just *as he was sent,* preaching and doing works, including healings, which act as signs given to elicit faith in Jesus.[45] The only requirement of the

---

43. Keener, *The Gospel of John,* 1204.

44. Ibid., 947. Keener suggests that the story of Elijah and Elisha is behind the giving of the Spirit and the disciples' ability to do greater works than Jesus. Before Elijah leaves, Elisha receives a double portion of Elijah's spirit. In 2 Kings, Elisha indeed does more and greater miracles than Elijah. Therefore, if the disciples are to receive the Spirit from Jesus, they will do his works and even greater ones than Jesus. Keener also sees a parallel between Jesus' words about "greater works" and Elisha's request for a double portion in his promise of the Paraclete in v. 16–17. John shows Jesus fulfilling the Elijah/Elisha motif with his disciples in John 20:22.

45. Reading John's commission here in John 20:21 in light of John 14:12, Randy Clark comments, "Essentially, Jesus was telling his disciples, 'What the Father sent me to do, *you* are going to do the same things.'" Clark, *Power to Heal,* 26.

Spirit-empowered disciples to do these works is faith: "He who believes in me will also do the works that I do . . ." (John 14:14).[46]

In the Synoptic Gospels, Jesus commissions his disciples both before and after his resurrection. Before his resurrection in Luke there are two separate commissions, one in which Jesus sends out the twelve and the other in which he sends out the seventy-two. In Matthew, Jesus charges the twelve to preach to the lost sheep of the house of Israel:

> And preach as you go, saying, 'The kingdom of heaven is at hand. Heal the sick, raise the dead, cleanse lepers, cast out demons. You received without pay, give without pay. (Matt 10:7–8)

Jesus commands the disciples to do what he was doing: preach the kingdom and manifest that kingdom by healing and delivering people from evil spirits.[47] Accordingly, in his commentary on Matthew, Craig Keener notes that the mission of Jesus is replicated and extended in the mission of the disciples: "Matthew emphasizes the continuity between Jesus' mission and that of the disciples precisely because the model of ministry God had exemplified in Jesus remains important for Jesus' followers."[48]

Just as in the ministry of Jesus, the disciples' proclamation of the kingdom comes with the *demonstration* of that kingdom through healing and deliverance. According to Pope Benedict XVI, the ministry of healing is not accidental to the proclamation of the gospel; rather, healing is an *essential* dimension of the Christian mission. Commenting on the commission of the twelve he writes:

46. Commenting on this verse, Raymond Brown explains: "Belief in Jesus will bring to the Christian power from God to perform the same works that Jesus performs, because, by uniting a man with Jesus and the Father, belief gives to him a share in the power that they possess." Raymond Brown, *The Gospel According to John 13–21*, 632.

47. According to the Doctrinal Commission of the ICCRS, these commissioning accounts reveal the intrinsic link between healing and evangelization: "In commissioning the apostles to continue his saving mission, Jesus reaffirms the intrinsic link between healing and the proclamation of the Gospel." Doctrinal Commission of the ICCRS, *Guidelines*, 31.

48. Keener, *Matthew*, 203.

> Healing is an essential dimension of the apostolic mission and of Christian faith in general . . . When understood at a sufficiently deep level, [healing] expresses the entire content of "redemption" . . . Healings are essentially "signs" that point to God himself and serve to set man in motion toward God . . . For Jesus himself and for his followers, miracles of healing are thus a subordinate element within the overall range of his activity, which is concerned with something deeper, with nothing less than the "kingdom of God": his becoming Lord in us and in the world.[49]

For Benedict, the physical healings that accompany the disciples' proclamation of the gospel have the function of orienting the hearers of the gospel toward God. The disciples' healings, therefore, have an *evangelistic purpose*; they are meant to engender faith in Jesus by which Jesus becomes Lord in the hearts of believers and the whole world. According to the CDF, "The power to heal is given [to the disciples] within a missionary context, not for their own exaltation, but to confirm their mission."[50] In this way, the evangelistic purpose of healings in the ministry of Jesus is paralleled and continued in the mission of the disciples.

Luke's version of the commissioning of the twelve, which is not limited to the Jews, is even more explicit: "Whenever you enter a town and they receive you, eat what is set before you; heal the sick in it and say to them, 'The kingdom of God has come near to you'" (Luke 9:1–2). At the end of Luke's commissioning account there is an important additional line: "And they departed and went through the villages, preaching the gospel and healing everywhere" (9:6). The disciples do what Jesus commands; they preach and heal just as he did.

Luke adds another commissioning account in which the Lord appoints and sends out ahead of him seventy-two additional disciples. Their commission is almost identical to that of the twelve: "Whenever you enter a town and they receive you; heal the sick

---

49. Pope Benedict XVI, *Jesus of Nazareth*, 176.

50. CDF, *Instruction on Prayers for Healing*, sec I, no. 3.

in it and say to them, 'The kingdom of God has come near to you'" (Luke 10:9). Here we can see that the words and deeds of the kingdom come together precisely in order to manifest that the kingdom of God has *come near*. It is the acceptance or rejection of this two-part proclamation of the kingdom that represents entry into or rejection of the kingdom.[51]

Alan Richardson summarizes the important role healing has in the preaching of the gospel in the commissioning accounts:

> The charge which was given by Jesus to his disciples as he sent them forth on their mission is reported four times in the Synoptic Gospels and on each occasion the commission to heal is placed alongside of the commission to preach (Mark 6:7–13; Matt 9:35–10:23; Luke 9:1–6, 10:1–20) . . . From the earliest days the ministry of healing was placed side by side with that of preaching in the missionary labours of the Church.[52]

Jesus very clearly intends to send his disciples to preach and to heal the sick. There is no distinction among these tasks; they go together.

The post-Resurrection account of the so-called Great Commission of Matthew 28, however, seems to conspicuously leave out any mention of healing and deliverance as part of the mission of the disciples:

> All authority in heaven and on earth been given to me. Go therefore and make disciples of all nations, baptizing them in the name of the Father and of the Son and of the Holy Spirit, teaching them to observe all that I have commanded you; and behold, I am with you always, to the close of the age. (Matt 28:18–20)

---

51. Like Matthew 11, Jesus' instruction to the disciples to shake the dust from their feet in a town that refuses to receive the kingdom indicates judgment, "I tell you, it shall be more tolerable on that day for Sodom than for that town" (10:12). The two-part gospel of the kingdom has been presented and rejected, and therefore judgment comes upon them.

52. Richardson, *The Miracle Stories of the Gospels*, 41–42.

This passage depicts Jesus as the Son of Man who fulfills the prophecies of Daniel 7:13-14 and has obtained plenary royal authority through his death and resurrection.[53] Before he ascends into heaven, Jesus entrusts this authority to his disciples so they might carry out his mission. Theologically speaking, the mission here is *making disciples*, a work that entails the *sacraments* (here baptism) and *teaching*. Thus, it seems there is nothing implicit or explicit here about healing the sick.[54] This commission, however, if read in light of the previous commissions of Jesus, needs to be understood as including healing the sick. In fact, there are several reasons why the Great Commission needs to be read in light of the previous commissions.

The first reason is that scholars understand the earlier commissions as *paradigmatic* for the commissioning of the believers in the Great Commission of Matthew 28. If this is true, then the Great Commission, while universal, at least is meant to include the content of the previous commissions, even if it is not explicit.[55] This means that the command to heal the sick in the former is still in force in the latter.

The second reason concerns the *authority* that Jesus entrusts to his disciples. The authority to carry out the Great Commission must be related to and *include* the authority Jesus gave to his disciples to heal the sick and drive out demons in the previous commissioning accounts.[56] In fact, the Greek word for authority (ἐξουσία) in the earlier commission accounts is the same word used in Matthew 28 (Matt 10:1; Luke 9:1, 10:1). Therefore, while the Great Commission does not explicitly command healing the sick, the textual evidence allows us to conclude firmly that it includes Jesus' earlier command to heal the sick and deliver people from evil spirits.

---

53. Keener, *Matthew*, 370.

54. This explicit omission in Matthew 28 has led some interpreters to conclude that the command to heal the sick and drive out demons is not a command for all believers. Ruthven, *What's Wrong with Protestant Theology?*, 211.

55. Ibid., 203–40.

56. Clark, *The Essential Guide to the Power*, 113.

The final reason this commission at the end of Matthew needs to be read in light of the prior accounts is that the mission to make disciples of all nations involves teaching them "to observe *all* that I have commanded you." If we look at the Gospel of Matthew, for example, what did Jesus command his disciples to do? Among other things, he commanded them to "preach the kingdom" and "heal the sick, raise the dead, cleanse lepers, and cast out demons" (Matt 10:7–8). In his book *Healing Ministry*, Jack Moraine describes the relationship between Jesus' command to teach in the Great Commission and his prior command to heal the sick and drive out demons:

> The point I wish to emphasize is that for Jesus' original audience—the twelve—the command to teach new disciples "to obey everything I have commanded you" had to include what Jesus commanded them in Matthew 10 concerning authority to heal and drive out demons. They were to teach new converts to obey what Jesus commanded them about healing the sick and demonized. Teaching followers of Jesus that they have been entrusted by Christ with authority to heal is part of basic training for the disciples. It is one aspect of what is involved in making disciples in fulfillment of the Great Commission.[57]

This interpretation of Matthew's post-Resurrection commission is consistent with Jesus' words about signs of healing in Mark's version of the Great Commission, where Jesus says:

> Go into all the world and preach the gospel to the whole creation. He who believes and is baptized will be saved; but he who does not believe will be condemned. And these signs will accompany those who believe: in my name they will cast out demons; they will speak in new tongues; they will pick up serpents, and if they

---

57. Moraine, *Healing Ministry*, 50. Randy Clark and Bob Sawvelle make a similar point. If the disciples are carrying on the mission of Jesus and if Jesus is telling them to teach them to observe everything he commanded them, then healing the sick, something that Jesus did frequently and taught them, has to be near the top of the list. See Clark, *Essential Guide*, 124, 182; and Sawvelle, *A Case for Healing Today*, 46.

> drink any deadly thing, it will not hurt them; they will
> lay their hands on the sick and they will recover. (Mark
> 16:17–18)[58]

The command to preach the gospel is accompanied by Jesus'
words regarding the supernatural signs of his power and presence
that will accompany those who believe in that preaching. When
the gospel is preached by the disciples, the sign of healing will be
present among those who believe. Thus, if the sign of healing is
not present among those who believe, then there is something not
present that Jesus indicated will be. Mary Healy explains how this
applies to believers as they preach the gospel:

> As the Twelve had done earlier (Mark 6:13), the believers
> will lay hands on the sick for healing. Just as Jesus always
> accompanied his preaching of the gospel with works of
> healing and deliverance (1:34, 3:10), so is the Church
> called to do. The preaching of the gospel is not merely
> verbal activity but a demonstration of God's power.[59]

Unlike Matthew, Mark includes the post-ascension preaching
of the gospel that shows that signs of healing indeed accompanied
the disciples as they preached the gospel:

> And they went forth and preached everywhere, while the
> Lord worked with them and confirmed the message by
> the signs that attended it. (Mark 16:20)

Not only does this ending demonstrate that our reading of
Matthew's post-resurrection commission is consistent with Mark,
but it also emphasizes a clearer relationship between Jesus' commission of the disciples to preach and signs of healing. R.T. France
believes verse 20 "summarizes the whole of the book of Acts in

---

58. While many scholars hold that Mark's original Gospel ended in 16:8,
this "second" ending (16:8–20) is nevertheless accepted as part of the canon of
Scripture by Christians. Healy, *Gospel of Mark*, 331.

59. Ibid., 334. Randy Clark writes, "If the commission to preach the gospel
is still in effect for believers (which is accepted everywhere), the sign that they
will lay hands on the sick and the sick will recover is also still in effect for
believers." Clark, *Global Awakening Ministry Team Training Manual*, 51.

a nutshell."[60] The similarity between the ending of Mark and the missionary activity of the disciples in Acts also leads Mary Beavis to suggest that another author added a final ending to Mark in order to show that the apostolic mission of the early church was "commanded by the Risen Jesus who still works together with them, and whose word is confirmed by powerful signs."[61] In Matthew, Jesus promises that he will be with them in their apostolic mission (Matt 28:20) and here in Mark we see just how the risen Lord accompanies them in their mission; he works with them and confirms their message through signs that include healing. Therefore, if we read the commissioning accounts together, we come to the unmistakable conclusion that Jesus' commands to preach the gospel and heal the sick are inseparable.

Summary and Conclusion

From the considerations above, we can conclude that there is an *intrinsic link* between evangelization and physical healings in the ministry of Jesus. Like the multiple strands of a strong rope, there are multiple individual links between preaching the gospel and healing that together form an inseparable connection. The first discernable link is evident in Jesus' proclamation of the inbreaking kingdom of God. The "already but not yet" nature of the kingdom of God through Jesus' proclamation gives us the theological understanding as to why deeds of healing accompany the proclamation of the kingdom. Further, as Jesus declares that God's reign has come, the deliverances and healings by which God delivers man from bondage to the devil demonstrate the presence of that kingdom. Without such concrete demonstrations, Jesus' proclamation that "the time is fulfilled" and "the kingdom of God is at hand" would seem empty to his audience. In other words, it is precisely because the kingdom of God has come in Jesus, that deliverances and healings accompany his preaching of the gospel of the kingdom. The

---

60. France, *The Gospel of Mark*, 687.

61. Beavis, *Mark*, 249.

proclamation of the gospel has a tangible but provisional effect upon the hearers of the gospel in order to demonstrate and express the truth of what is proclaimed. Healings and deliverances serve as signs of the inbreaking presence of the kingdom that point to the deeper truth of the kingdom of God: that God is reconciling man to himself in Jesus. *Therefore, the healings that accompany the proclamation of the kingdom not only demonstrate that kingdom, but they also confirm the truth of the message of the kingdom, which is a message of eternal salvation in Christ.*

This leads us to the next link: *healings are signs meant to elicit faith in Jesus as the Messiah and Son of God.* The mission of the Messiah in the Spirit, according to the Old Testament, includes the preaching of the good news and deeds of healing and deliverance. The prophetic mission of the Messiah has two parts, words and deeds, which are inextricably united in the ministry of Jesus. The presence of these deeds is so constitutive of his anointing that he uses them as evidence that he is the Messiah when asked by disciples of John the Baptist. These deeds, therefore, serve as signs of his identity as the long-awaited Messiah. But even more importantly, these messianic deeds of healing are signs given for the purpose of *faith* in Jesus as the Son of God. Jesus' rebuke of the unbelief of Bethsaida and Chorazin proves that his healings and mighty works are given precisely for the purpose of repentance and faith in him. Furthermore, in many places in the Gospel of John, the "works" and healings of Jesus point to his identity as the Son of God. In this way, the works of Jesus serve as signs for the purpose of eliciting faith that he is from God, since only someone from God could do such things. If Jesus does such things, the only proper response is repentance and faith.

Next, *healings and testimonies of healings play a significant role in drawing people to come to Jesus.* Jesus' miracles and healings initially draw people to Jesus who then hear the good news in his preaching. The effect is that large crowds of people hear the gospel for the first time. Moreover, the testimony of those who experience healing or witness healings also draws many people to come to Jesus and to approach him in faith. Without the healings that accompany the ministry of Jesus as depicted in the Gospels, it is almost inconceivable that he would have attracted so many to hear the good news and subsequently respond to him with repentance and faith. Testimonies of healings, therefore, not only draw people to Jesus, they also serve to open people's hearts to hear what Jesus has to say about the kingdom.

The next strong link between the preaching of the gospel and healing is found in the commissioning accounts of the disciples of Jesus, where *we discover the inseparability of the command to preach and the command to heal.* In the Gospel of John, the risen Jesus breathes on his disciples and sends his disciples out just as he was sent: preaching and doing the works of healing that he did and greater ones in the power of the Spirit. In the synoptic accounts of the commissioning, the disciples are commanded to do what Jesus was doing: to proclaim the kingdom, drive out evil spirits, and heal people of their sicknesses. While each Synoptic Gospel portrays this commission differently, the evangelists intentionally show Jesus entrusting his authority to his disciples so they can continue his mission of proclaiming and demonstrating the kingdom of God by healing the sick. If the accounts are considered together, we can even see in the post-ascension "Great Commission" accounts of Matthew and Mark the clear command to the early church to continue the ministry of preaching, healing, and delivering people from evil spirits.

Finally, the connection between healing and preaching the gospel in the commissioning is especially clear in the final chapter of Mark, where healing is not only one of the signs that will accompany those who believe in the gospel, but also a sign that the Lord Jesus is present with his disciples as they proclaim the gospel. Most importantly, the final verse of Mark's commission narrative is perhaps the clearest in the Synoptic Gospels regarding the relationship between the proclamation of the gospel and healing. There, the disciples' preaching of the gospel is to be permeated by the power and presence of the Lord Jesus who confirms the message of the gospel through the sign of healing the sick. *Therefore, the healings that accompany the preaching of the gospel function precisely to confirm the validity and power of the gospel message itself.* This very theme is continued in the Acts of the Apostles to which we now turn.

Chapter 2

Healing and Evangelization
in the Acts of the Apostles

IN ORDER FOR THE disciples to fulfill the mission that Jesus gives to them, the evangelists, each in his own way, account for the power and presence of Jesus among them as they go forth to preach the gospel. In John's commissioning account, as we noted above, Jesus breathes on his disciples thereby imparting to them his Spirit so they can continue his mission and do the works he did and greater ones (John 20:22). After Jesus commissions the disciples in Matthew, he gives to them the authority he received from the Father and promises he will be with them always (Matt 28:20). After the ascension, Mark shows Jesus' powerful presence with the disciples as they preached: "And they went forth and preached everywhere, while the Lord worked with them and confirmed the message by the signs that attended it" (Mark 16:20). In each of the three gospels above, the authors theologically account for the power that animates the disciples' mission which includes both words and deeds.

It is above all in Luke's gospel and in his Acts of the Apostles that the connection between the mission of Jesus and the mission of the disciples comes into clearest focus. In the first two verses of Acts, Luke writes, "In the first book, O Theophilus, I have dealt with all that *Jesus began to do and teach*, after he had given commandment through the Holy Spirit to the apostles he had chosen" (Acts 1:1–2, emphasis mine). With this phrase, Luke intends to show that there is a *continuation* of Jesus' ministry in and through the church. Luke will later show that the Spirit that empowered Jesus for mission is the same Spirit that empowers the disciples to witness to Jesus. In part one of this chapter we will briefly examine the essential *theological link* between the anointing of Jesus and the anointing of the disciples at Pentecost, and establish that such ministry was expected to be continued in the church. In part two we will examine the role of "signs and wonders" and healings in the proclamation of the gospel in the Acts of the Apostles. From this we can gain a better understanding of the relationship between the empowered preaching of the gospel and deeds of healing in the apostolic church.

Pentecost and the Mission of Jesus in the Church

Before his ascension in Luke, Jesus commands his disciples to preach the gospel to the world. Jesus, however, tells his disciples first to *wait* in Jerusalem until they are "clothed with power" to fulfill their mission to preach to the whole world: "Behold, I send the promise of my Father upon you; but stay in the city until you are clothed with power from on high" (Luke 24:49). Jesus says virtually the same thing in Acts 1:4–5:

> And while staying with them he charged them not to depart from Jerusalem, but to wait for the promise of the Father which, he said, "you heard from me, for John baptized with water, but before many days you shall be baptized with the Holy Spirit. (Acts 1:4-5)

In order for them to fulfill the mission he gave them, the disciples need to be clothed with power and "baptized in the Spirit." In each of the Gospels, Jesus is depicted as the one who will "baptize in the Spirit" (Mark 1:8; Matt 3:11; Luke 3:16; John 1:33). According to Luke, the disciples need to be baptized in the Spirit by

Jesus in order to fulfill their mission to bear witness to him. This is precisely what happens at Pentecost (Acts 2:1–13).

In Luke-Acts, the anointing the disciples receive at Pentecost for mission is closely linked to the anointing Jesus receives at his baptism for his mission. Charles Talbert, in fact, shows that the anointing of Jesus in his baptism has a fourfold parallel to the disciples' baptism in the Spirit at Pentecost:

1. Jesus and the disciples praying,

2. the Spirit descends after their prayers,

3. there is a physical manifestation of the Spirit, and

4. the ministries of both Jesus and the disciples begin with a sermon that is thematic of what follows . . .[1]

The close parallels show, according to Roger Stronstad, the *functional equivalence* between the two events in the narrative of the rest of each book respectively:

> Therefore, since the gift of the Spirit to Jesus inaugurates and empowers his mission, then, whatever meaning Spirit baptism might have in other contexts, it has the same primary charismatic meaning for the mission of the disciples as the anointing by the Spirit had for the charismatic mission of Jesus.[2]

The powerful effects of Jesus' baptism are demonstrated through his Spirit-empowered ministry of preaching, healing, and delivering people from evil.[3] The theological framework in which to understand this ministry in Luke is given in Jesus' inaugural preaching in Luke 4, where he associates the deeds that accompany his messianic mission with the anointing of the Spirit.

The connection between Jesus' anointing and his mighty deeds is clear in Acts 10:38, where Peter preaches to the house of

1. Stronstad, *The Charismatic Theology of St. Luke*, 58.

2. Ibid., 58.

3. Shelton, *Mighty in Word and Deed*, 48–49. See also Doctrinal Commission of Catholic Charismatic Renewal Services (ICCRS), *Baptism of the Holy Spirit*, 25.

Cornelius and speaks about "how God anointed Jesus of Nazareth with the Holy Spirit and with power; how he went about doing good and healing all that were oppressed by the devil, for God was with him."[4] According to Stronstad, the same framework that describes the power in Jesus' ministry in terms of the Spirit also describes the powerful ministry of the disciples in terms of Pentecost: "Just as the mission of Jesus was inaugurated in the power of the Spirit, so at Pentecost the mission of the disciples will be inaugurated in the power of the Spirit."[5] This is why the same miraculous activity of Jesus is predicated of the disciples after Pentecost: "And fear came upon every soul: and many wonders and signs were done through the apostles" (Acts 2:43). The same Spirit-empowered deeds that marked Jesus' ministry are continued in the early church.[6] According to Raniero Cantalamessa, Pentecost is the interpretive key for understanding the apostolic activity in Acts in the same way that the anointing of Jesus at his baptism is the interpretive key for understanding Jesus' Spirit-empowered activity in Luke's gospel.[7]

If the anointing of Jesus at his baptism and the anointing of the disciples at Pentecost are the functional equivalent of each other in Luke-Acts, then we can understand more fully the *theological connection* Luke is making between what Jesus did in his earthly ministry and the mission of the disciples.[8] In baptizing

4. In his Pentecost sermon, Peter also describes Jesus of Nazareth as "a man attested to you by God with mighty works and wonders and signs which God did through him in your midst" (Acts 2:22).

5. Stronstad, *The Charismatic Theology*, 59, 81.

6. Shelton puts it this way: "The architecture that Luke provides for the Gospel and Acts makes a strong statement: the common denominator between the acts of Jesus and acts of the apostles is the power of the Holy Spirit . . . The Spirit-anointed Jesus performed miracles and poured out this same Spirit on the believers; therefore his church is endowed to perform God's wonders." Shelton, *Mighty and Word and Deed*, 82.

7. Cantalamessa, *The Holy Spirit in the Life of Jesus*, 12.

8. Regarding the words and deeds of Jesus being present in the early church, James Shelton writes: "Knowing that the believers received from Jesus the same Holy Spirit that empowered him, Luke expects that the Spirit-words and Spirit-works will continue in the church." Shelton, *Mighty and Word in Deed*, 81.

the disciples with his Spirit at Pentecost, Jesus gives the disciples a share in his own messianic anointing of the Spirit so that Jesus can continue his mission in and through the apostolic church by means of the Spirit. This theological connection is what accounts for the church's bold preaching and ability to perform signs, wonders, and healings.[9]

The outpouring of the Spirit at Pentecost in Acts 2:1–2 is so central to Jesus' mission in the church that Jesus also gives the disciples a new understanding of the kingdom of God based on this outpouring. In response to his disciples' question about the coming of God's kingdom Jesus says:

> It is not for you to know times or seasons which the Father has fixed by his own authority. But you shall receive power when the Holy Spirit has come upon you; and you shall be my witnesses in Jerusalem and in all Judea and Samaria and to the end of the earth. (Acts 1:7–8)

In responding in this way, Jesus interprets the presence of the kingdom in terms of the Holy Spirit's activity in the mission of the church.[10] Thus, the event of Pentecost directly relates the kingdom of God preached by Jesus to the era of the church. The kingdom of God made present in and through Jesus' ministry is now made present through the Spirit who empowers both the church's preaching and miracles.[11] O'Reilly too understands Pentecost as

9. O'Reilly, *Word and Sign*, 17.

10. Montague, *The Holy Spirit*, 269, 273.

11. Youngmo Cho, in his doctoral dissertation, examines the relationship between the Spirit and the kingdom of God in the writings of Paul and Luke. He concludes that the Spirit in Luke-Acts is not identical to the presence of the kingdom but is closely related to the power to proclaim and make it present. "The anointing of the Spirit upon Jesus is primarily linked to his carrying out this messianic commission in terms of the proclamation of the good news of the kingdom of God. Similarly, one of the main themes of the church's proclamation in Acts is consistently presented as the kingdom of God . . . Furthermore, just as the Spirit is the main source of power of Jesus' proclamation, the Spirit is still at work in the Church's proclaiming of the kingdom. The disciples' mission to witness to Jesus and the kingdom is accomplished by their Spirit-empowerment so extending the kingdom beyond Israel." Cho, *Spirit and Kingdom in the Writings of Luke and Paul*, 195.

the anointing given to the disciples for the purpose of their mission in proclaiming the kingdom:

> When Luke describes the Pentecost event as a baptism of the disciples, he is pointing first of all to its character as the inaugural event of the apostolic mission. He is relating it to the baptism of Jesus and so suggesting that it has a similar import to that event, namely, the prophetic anointing of the apostles for their mission of preaching the kingdom of God and inaugurating that kingdom by means of miracles of healing and exorcism.[12]

The pentecostal Spirit poured out on the early church is the source of power for the disciples to do what Jesus did in the Gospels. Just as Jesus proclaimed the kingdom of God in word and demonstrated it through the deeds of healing and deliverance by the power of the Spirit, the apostles, now anointed by the same Spirit, can witness to him as Jesus confirms their message through deeds. These deeds—signs, wonders, and healings—accompany the spread of the gospel at every turn in Acts.

Healing and the Spread of the Gospel

There are two general ways Luke speaks about healing and the proclamation of the gospel in Acts: (1) the performance of signs, wonders, and healings in the context of preaching the gospel, and (2) individual stories of healings which lead to the preaching of the gospel. Both lead to an increase of believers and the spread of the gospel. In this section, we will consider how signs, wonders, and healings function in Acts in relationship with the preaching of the gospel by examining select passages where they are coordinated with each other.

In the Old Testament, the term "signs and wonders" often refers to the miraculous demonstrations of God's saving power to Israel in the exodus. As signs, these miracles pointed to and

12. O'Reilly, *Word and Sign*, 53.

confirmed God's presence among his people.[13] In the Acts of the Apostles, Luke also uses this phrase with a similar meaning. The phrases "signs and wonders" (σημεῖα καὶ τέρατα) and "wonders and signs" (τέρατα καὶ σημεῖα) are used ten times in the Acts of the Apostles and their meaning becomes clear by the context in which they occur.[14] These words first appear in the Pentecost preaching of Peter as he quotes from Joel 2 describing the eschatological outpouring of the Spirit of prophecy upon the church. Peter adds the word "wonders" to the line of Joel, "I will show *wonders* in the heaven above and signs on the earth beneath, blood, and fire, and vapor of smoke" (2:19, emphasis mine). George Montague believes the addition of "wonders" to this prophecy of Joel is significant for understanding God's work in Pentecost and in the early church:

> The result of the change [Luke adding the word wonders to signs] is that an apocalyptic statement about the end-time is changed into a prophetic Mosaic-exodus statement. The expression "signs and wonders" *(sēmeia kai terata)* is a stereotyped Septuagint expression for the marvelous deeds worked by God through Moses in bringing the people out of Egypt (Ex 7:3, etc.). The order, of course, here is reversed to "wonders and signs," but this is even more significant, for it points us to the one place in the Septuagint where the order is also reversed in the same way: "[Wisdom] entered the Lord's servant and withstood mighty kings with wonders and signs (*en terasi kai sēmeios*)" and "made the tongues of those who could not speak eloquent . . . and prospered their works by the hand of the holy prophet" (Wis 10:16–11:1).[15]

From this, Montague argues on the one hand that Luke modifies Joel's prophecy in order to point to Pentecost as a wonder from

13. Hahn, *Catholic Bible Dictionary*, 846. See Exod 4:8–9, 17, 28, 39; 7:3; 10:1; Num 14:11, 22; Deut 4:34; 7:19; 26:8; 29:3; 34:11; Josh 24:17; Neh 9:10; Ps 78:43; 105:27; 135:9; Jer 32:20).

14. The phrase "wonders and signs" is found in Acts 2:22, 2:43; 6:8; 7:36. The phrase "signs and wonders" is found in Acts 4:30; 5:12; 14:3; and 15:12. In Acts 2:19, Luke adds the word "wonders" to Joel's prophecy.

15. Montague, *The Holy Spirit*, 285–86.

heaven that indicates the imminence of the day of the Lord and a call for conversion. But on the other hand, Montague understands the new phrase "wonders and signs" as pointing forward to the coming "wonders and signs" that will be worked through the early church in Jesus' name.[16] Either way, the phrase "signs and wonders" recalls God's salvific activity that demonstrates his presence among his people.

Since it is God alone who can perform signs and wonders, Luke's use of the phrase indicates an *intentional association* of those who perform them with God's presence. In the latter part of his Pentecost sermon, Peter describes Jesus as a man "attested to you by God with mighty works and wonders and signs which God did through him" (Acts 2:22). By noting the supernatural works of Jesus, Peter essentially argues that Jesus' signs and wonders constitute a kind of verification of his identity as Lord.[17] If Jesus' signs and wonders point to his identity, then it is significant that Luke in the same chapter shows that Jesus' works are continued in the apostolic church: "And fear came upon every soul; and many wonders and signs were done through the apostles" (Acts 2:42). Luke seems to intentionally link the ministry of Jesus to the ministry of the apostles for the purpose of accrediting the apostolic church. Warrington notes:

> [The healings of the disciples] are closely linked to those of Jesus, demonstrating that they are messengers following his example, walking in his footsteps, but also that Jesus is present among them . . . the work of the Apostles is still the work of Jesus—God is the agent of both. The healings do not just validate them and their ministries; they are also to be understood as continually validating

16. Ibid., 286. William Kurz agrees: "Earthly wonders and signs recall the miracles that God worked through Moses to free the Israelites from slavery in Egypt (Exod 7:3; Deut 4:34) and the miracles worked by Jesus in his public ministry (Acts 2:22). Wonders in the heavens are typical in biblical prophecies of the last day, the day when God would intervene in history to destroy evil and restore the fortunes of his people (Isa 13:10, Ezek 32:7; Rev 6:12). Kurz, *Acts of the Apostles*, 52.

17. Ibid., 54.

the person and ministry of Jesus in the present insofar as
the miracles are presented as being the ongoing work of
the risen Lord, albeit through the Apostles.[18]

The signs and wonders in the early church, therefore, not only serve to validate the message and ministry of the apostolic church, but also to confirm that the risen Jesus is present in the church and working in it. This evidence of the presence and power of Jesus is critically important for the nascent church as it proclaims him.

The strong link between Jesus' continual presence in the church through signs and wonders and the proclamation of the gospel is evident in the apostolic church's prayer before the "little Pentecost" of Acts 4. After Peter and John are released from jail, the community as a whole comes together to implore God: "And now, Lord, look upon their threats, and grant to your servants to speak your word with all boldness, while you stretch out your hand to heal, and signs and wonders are performed through the name of your holy servant Jesus" (Acts 4:29–31). The prayer of the disciples contains three petitions: (1) that God look upon their threats, (2) that the church be able to speak the word with all boldness, and (3) that the Lord heal and perform signs and wonders through the name of Jesus. Instead of merely praying for more boldness to proclaim the gospel, the apostles ask for more boldness in preaching *and* for the Lord to confirm their preaching with miracles. According to Shelton, the latter two petitions are closely related. The apostles pray for the ability to preach the word with all boldness because they understand their primary task is to preach the gospel (word), but they also pray that God will work signs, wonders, and healings (deeds) because it is the responsibility of the risen Lord, who is present among them, to confirm their message.[19] *Essentially, the disciples pray both for boldness in preaching and for healings, signs, and wonders because they believe both are needed for them to witness effectively to the risen Jesus.* Just as signs and wonders were done through the apostles as they bore witness to Jesus after receiving the Spirit at Pentecost (Acts 2:42), so the

18. Warrington, "Acts and the Healing Narratives," 198.

19. Shelton, *Mighty in Word and Deed,* 82.

prayer of the apostolic church in the "little Pentecost" increases its signs and wonders in order to bear witness to Jesus throughout Acts.

According to Robert Gallagher, Luke shows how the petitions in Acts 4 are answered in the narrative that follows. Gallagher maintains that God's answer to the petition for more signs, wonders, and healings to accompany their bold preaching becomes explicit in the summary Luke offers of the success of apostolic evangelization in Jerusalem.[20]

> Now many signs and wonders were done among the people by the hands of the apostles. And they were all together in Solomon's Portico. None of the rest dared join them, but the people held them in high honor. And more than ever believers were added to the Lord, multitudes both of men and women, so that they even carried out the sick into the streets, and laid them on beds and pallets, that as Peter came by at least his shadow might fall on some of them. The people also gathered from the towns around Jerusalem bringing the sick and those afflicted with unclean spirits, and they were all healed. (Acts 5:12–16)

While the exact relationship between the proclamation of the gospel and these healings is not clear from this passage, it nonetheless gives us a strong indication of the intrinsic correlation between the two. It is in the context of describing the apostles' signs and wonders that Luke notes that *multitudes* of "believers were added to the Lord." If Luke indeed is intentionally describing the apostolic ministry as patterned after Jesus' ministry as we noted above, then it is reasonable to conclude that the healings in this passage function in a similar way as they did in Jesus' ministry; they demonstrate the truth of the message and serve as effective signs of God's presence. Moreover, Luke recounts clearly the reason why many people are drawn to the apostolic church when he notes that the multitudes were bringing their sick to the church for

---

20. Gallagher, "From 'Doingness' to 'Beingness,'" 52–53.

healing.[21] Because these healings were drawing so many people to the apostles, as is evident in this passage, they provide a "massive evangelizing momentum" for the apostolic church.[22] This is especially clear in verse 16, which notes that the healings drew people from the neighboring towns around Jerusalem who had not yet heard the gospel. Other than the news of what happened at Pentecost in Acts 2:9, this is the first time the gospel reaches beyond Jerusalem into Judea in Acts.[23] In this way, the signs of healing that accompany the gospel are a significant factor in the growth of the early church.

Warrington, in fact, understands that healings in Acts serve as "launch pads" for new mission territory for the apostolic church as foretold by Jesus in Acts 1:8: "But you shall receive power when the Spirit has come upon you; and you shall be my witnesses in Jerusalem and in all Judea and Samaria and to the ends of the earth." Warrington notes that the healing activity of the apostles serves to transition the church's evangelization into new geographical areas. The healing of the lame man at the temple gate (Acts 3:1–10) leads Peter to preach to the Jews in Jerusalem, many of whom come to believe (Acts 4:4). As noted above, the healings in this passage (5:12–16) lead to preaching to those in Judea, many of whom are then added to the Lord.[24] The healings at the hands of Philip in Samaria lead to the preaching and spread of the gospel in Samaria (Acts 8:4–8). Finally, Paul's missionary efforts (Acts 14:3, 8–10, 19–20) mark the beginnings of the gospel spreading to the Gentiles.[25] Warrington concludes that "the agenda set by the Spirit and recorded by Luke is developed through Acts, healings helping to open the door into new communities from Jerusalem outwards."[26] Consequently, healings in Acts function as "launch

---

21. Craig Keener notes that healings in Acts are the main means of drawing crowds to hear the gospel. Keener, *The Spirit in the Gospels and Acts,* 209.

22. Kurz, *Acts of the Apostles,* 99.

23. Dunn, *The Acts of the Apostle,* 66.

24. Ibid., 66.

25. Warrington, "Acts and the Healing Narratives," 196–97.

26. Ibid., 197.

pads," or events from which the gospel is preached credibly and effectively in new territory.

In chapter 6, the spirit of wisdom manifested in the preaching of Stephen is associated with his performing of signs and wonders. "Stephen, full of grace and power, did great wonders and signs among the people . . . But they could not withstand the wisdom and the Spirit with which he spoke" (Acts 6:8, 10). The presence of the Spirit that gives him wisdom in preaching is also the source of his ability to do great wonders and signs. After Stephen's martyrdom, which brings about strong persecution, Philip goes to proclaim Christ in Samaria, where the connection between preaching and healing is particularly clear:

> Philip went down to a city in Samaria, and proclaimed to them the Christ. And the multitude with one accord gave heed to what was said by Philip, when they heard him and saw the signs which he did. For unclean spirits came out of many who were possessed, crying with a loud voice; and many who were paralyzed or lame were healed. So there was much joy in that city. (Acts 8:5–8)

A couple of conclusions can be drawn from this passage. First, the link between the preaching of Christ and healing is explicit here: the Samaritans gave heed to the message of the gospel precisely when they heard Philip *and* saw the signs he did. On the one hand, there was something about the *manner* in which Philip was preaching. This is not surprising since Luke describes Philip and the other seven servants in Acts 6:3 as "full of the Spirit and of wisdom." That Spirit-filled preaching has a powerful effect on listeners is clear in the example of Stephen (6:10). But, on the other hand, the signs of healing and deliverance in verse 7 give explicit *credibility* to the gospel message itself. The Spirit-filled preaching of Philip accompanied by signs and wonders—in particular healings and exorcisms—caused the Samaritans to give heed to what he said. This is all the more important in light of the fact that Philip encounters Simon the magician (8:9–13) who formerly amazed the people with his signs.

Second, the signs Philip performs do not primarily function as that which validate him as an accredited preacher of the gospel. Instead, the text says the Samaritans "gave heed to *what was said by Philip*." This is later confirmed in 8:12–13: "But when they believed Philip as he preached good news about the kingdom of God and the name of Jesus, they were baptized, both men and women." Parsons explains:

> So to preach the gospel for Philip was to proclaim that Jesus was the "Christ," the one God had anointed "for doing good and healing all who were oppressed by the devil" (as Peter would put it in 10:38). Hence Philip's signs and wonders—healings and exorcisms—were outward signs reinforcing his message: Satan is being overcome, and the kingdom of God is being established.[27]

This passage is thus another instance of what we see in Mark 16:20, where Jesus works signs to confirm the message of the gospel. Since signs of healing also function in Acts to confirm the message, then theoretically anyone who preaches the gospel, not just apostles, can see signs that accompany their message.[28]

In chapter 9, Peter's healing of the paralyzed man who had been bedridden for eight years at Lydda plays a large role in the conversion of more than one town. The explicit words of Peter indicate that Christ was proclaimed as he healed the man: "Aeneas, Jesus Christ heals you; rise and make your bed" (9:34). This healing has a wide-ranging effect: "And all the residents of Lydda and Sharon saw him, and they turned to the Lord" (9:35). James Dunn explains that

> the effect of the cure (9:35) is consistent both with what might have been expected and with Luke's consistent emphasis on the faith-generating effect of miracles. 'All the residents' means all Jews, since the towns were Jewish. 'Turned to the Lord' . . . becomes one of Luke's principal ways of describing conversion.[29]

---

27. Parsons, *Acts*, 115.

28. This topic will be covered in more detail in chapter 4.

29. Dunn, *The Acts of the Apostles*, 129.

In these few verses, healing functions as that which opens people to the truth of the gospel message about Jesus. Or as Dunn puts it, healings that accompany the gospel are "faith-generating" and, therefore, have the capacity to lead to belief in the message of the gospel.

Another clear connection between preaching and signs and wonders appears when Paul and Barnabas come to the Jewish town of Iconium: "So they remained for a long time, speaking boldly for the Lord, who bore witness to the word of his grace, granting signs and wonders to be done by their hands" (14:3). Paul and Barnabas preach boldly and the Lord bears witness to the preached word by granting signs and wonders. In the same chapter, Paul heals a cripple from birth while he is preaching (14:8–11). Evidently, preaching and healing were associated enough in Paul's mind that "seeing that he has the faith to be well," Paul stops his preaching and heals the man on the spot (v. 9). The public response to this healing is so strong that the crowds believe Paul and Barnabas are the gods Hermes and Zeus. When unbelieving Jews come from Antioch and Iconium, they persuade the crowds against them and stone Paul. The negative reaction to Paul's healing by unbelieving Jews exposes their unbelief just as it did in Jesus' ministry.[30]

In Paul's preaching in Ephesus we see yet another correlation between preaching and healing. Describing Paul's preaching in the synagogue, Luke says: "And [Paul] entered the synagogue and for three months spoke boldly, arguing and pleading about the kingdom of God" (19:8). But the people responded with unbelief and stubbornness to such a degree that Paul takes the disciples and moves his preaching to the hall of Tyrannus: "This continued for two years, so that all the residents of Asia heard the word of the Lord, both Jews and Greeks. And God did extraordinary miracles by the hands of Paul, so that handkerchiefs or aprons were carried away from his body to the sick, and diseases left them and evil spirits came out of them" (Acts 19:10–12). Paul's preaching too is

---

30. In other passages, healings result in opposition or misunderstanding: Acts 16:16–24; 19:11–16. Warrington, "Acts and the Healing Narratives," 190.

unmistakably linked with performing healings, the latter making fruitful the former.

Summary and Conclusion

The Acts of the Apostles gives us a privileged glimpse into the life of the early church and how it begins to fulfill the mission Jesus entrusted to it. At Pentecost, the disciples are baptized in the Spirit and given the power to witness to Jesus and preach the kingdom both in word (bold and inspired speech) and in deed (signs, wonders and healings). Luke sets forth this Spirit-empowered mission of the early church in deliberate parallel to Jesus' Spirit-empowered mission in his gospel, showing that the mission of Jesus is continued in the mission of the church. If in the life of Jesus the anointing of the Spirit gives him the power to preach the gospel with authority, heal the sick, and cast out demons, then the outpouring of the same Spirit at Pentecost will enable the disciples to do the same. The *theological connection* between the mission of Jesus and the commissioning accounts in the Synoptic Gospels is, therefore, rooted in the anointing of the Holy Spirit which empowered the nascent church to witness powerfully to Jesus. Significantly, there is nothing in Luke or Acts that implies that this anointing for mission is meant only for the apostolic period. The theological foundation for the mission of Jesus' preaching and healing to continue in the church is sealed in the Lukan corpus.

The signs, wonders, and healings made possible by this Pentecostal anointing function in various ways in the preaching of the gospel in Acts. *First, by showing that the disciples do signs and wonders just as Jesus did, Luke communicates powerfully that Jesus is indeed present in and with the church as they proclaim him.* This presence of the risen Jesus demonstrates a necessary continuity between the early church and Jesus who is preached. The disciples who proclaim Jesus are not, therefore, a rogue group of wonder-workers, but ambassadors of the risen Jesus who is alive and present among them. Put another way, the very Jesus who is preached as risen from the dead is manifested and still working his signs, wonders, and healings in and through the church he sent to proclaim him. In this sense, healings also affirm the authority of those who preach the gospel.[31]

This leads to another way healings function with regard to the preaching of the church: *they serve as signs which confirm the message of the gospel.* As the disciples share the gospel, the signs, wonders, and healings done by Jesus point to his presence with them and confirm the word they preach about him. When the kingdom of God is made visible through signs, wonders, and healings, the message of the kingdom is made more credible. *As a confirmation of the gospel message, healings have a powerful evangelistic purpose; they open people to faith in Jesus who is proclaimed.*[32] Kurz offers a succinct synthesis of this relationship between healing and the confirmation of the message in Acts:

> Through Acts, the proclamation of the good news is accompanied by healings and miracles done in the name of Jesus, who has divine power to do what is humanly impossible. During his earthly ministry, Jesus instructed his apostles to "proclaim the kingdom of God and to heal" the sick (Lk 9:2). Although miraculous healings are not necessary to faith, they play the important role of visibly manifesting the reality of the kingdom. They are signs demonstrating the truth of the gospel message: that God loves all people; that Jesus has won the victory over sin, sickness, and death; that he has come to heal and save. They thus dispose people's hearts to believe in the Lord Jesus, who is being proclaimed to them.[33]

---

31. Ibid., 215–16.

32. Ibid., 195. See also O'Reilly, *Word and Sign,* 134. O'Reilly also understands healings as signs that point to the resurrection of Jesus. He references Acts 3:15, where Peter explicitly links the proclamation of Jesus' resurrection with the healing of the lame man in 3:1–10. "The resurrection was the great miracle, the outstanding manifestation of God's power; the miracles, as further signs of that power, point to the resurrection. They extend that event into the time of the church and bear striking witness to its reality and actuality in the present." O'Reilly, *Word and Sign,* 139–40.

33. Kurz, *Acts of the Apostles,* 69–70.

The disciples are so aware of the evangelistic power of signs, wonders, and healings in their preaching, that in Acts 4 they beg God to *increase* them as they continue to bear witness to Jesus. *According to Acts, therefore, the presence of signs, wonders, and healings in the preaching of the gospel demonstrates the truth of the message of the gospel and thus disposes people to faith.* The powerful twofold gospel of word and deed is how Luke accounts for the fast spread and growth of the apostolic church.

Finally, in the proclamation of the gospel in Acts, *healings serve as major launch pads from which the church embarks into new mission territory.* Precisely because signs, wonders, and healings have the effect of drawing so many people to the church, people from new and uncharted territories that come for healing (and are healed) personally witness the word of the gospel confirmed and, as a result, open their hearts to the gospel. Therefore, the healings that Jesus performs in and through the church gives the church a "massive evangelizing momentum" that assists in opening the door to new areas for mission.

Chapter 3

Healing and Evangelization in the Letters of Paul

THERE ARE TWO FACTS that make an examination of the relationship between healing and evangelization difficult in Paul: (1) explicit references to healing in the Pauline corpus are much rarer than in the Gospels and Acts, and (2) we have a very limited understanding of the nature of Paul's initial proclamation of the gospel in his letters because they were written to address specific pastoral and theological issues. On the one hand, these two facts make it more difficult to tease out the precise relationship between preaching and healing. On the other hand, the fact that miracles and healings are not as pronounced in Paul's writings does not mean they were unimportant to Paul or that they did not play a significant role in the proclamation of the gospel.[1] In fact, closer

---

1. The marked contrast between the portrait of Paul in the Acts of the Apostles as a missionary who is a prolific miracle worker and the way he is depicted in his letters, as an intellectual pastor who is concerned largely with theological issues, is a well-known puzzle of biblical scholarship. The absence of much emphasis on miracles in Paul's letters has led some scholars to conclude (falsely) that there is a fundamental discontinuity between the miraculous ministry of Jesus and that of Paul. In his groundbreaking historical and biblical study *Paul and the Miraculous: A Historical Reconstruction*, Graham Twelftree attempts to reestablish the relationship Paul has with the miraculous. The result is a more balanced historical view of Paul in which the miraculous is

examination of the texts of Paul reveals that miracles and healings not only were present in the communities to which he wrote, but they also played an irreplaceable role in making the gospel he preached persuasive to his listeners. The first part of this chapter will examine a few principal passages where Paul addresses the *manner* in which his gospel came to the communities to which he preached: in power and the Holy Spirit. The second part of this chapter will briefly discuss the complex question of the charism of healing in 1 Corinthians 12 in terms of its relationship with evangelization in the New Testament. The charism will then be discussed in terms of Paul's exhortation to seek the "higher gifts" for the sake of evangelization and the building up the body of Christ.

The Gospel that Comes in Spirit and in Power

Paul understands the gospel in terms of *power*: "For I am not ashamed of the gospel; it is the power [δύναμις] of God for salvation to everyone who has faith" (Rom 1:16). While the word "power" here in Romans refers to the power of the gospel that leads to salvation in Christ, there are several key passages where Paul speaks about the power of the gospel both in terms of the *means by which it comes* and *its effects on his listeners as it is preached*.[2] Each of these key passages is significant as we consider the connection between healing and the preaching of the gospel.

---

brought back into its proper and fundamental place in his life and preaching. Twelftree, *Paul and the Miraculous*. Given the rigor of this recent study, we will follow it closely at times.

2. Frank Matera rightly understands the gospel having power in the sense that the proclamation of the gospel results in salvation. Matera, *Romans*, 34–35. The correlation between the gospel and power here and elsewhere in Paul's letters, however, has led some scholars to believe that there is an inherent relationship between the power of the gospel and the power that works miracles in such a way that one cannot be separated from the other. "While the plural *dunameis* throughout denotes miracles, the singular *dunamis* can, on the other hand, mean likewise the power which produces miracles as well as the power and the Spirit which the miracles reveal." Greig, *The Kingdom and the Power*, 137. For a detailed discussion as to how the singular δύναμις can refer to miracle power in Paul, see Twelftree, *Paul and the Miraculous*, 183–87.

One of the most relevant passages about the relationship between the proclamation of the gospel and healing is 1 Corinthians 2:1–5, where Paul describes the means by which his proclamation came to the Corinthians:

> When I came to you, brethren, I did not come proclaiming to you the testimony of God in lofty words or wisdom. For I decided to know nothing among you except Jesus Christ and him crucified. And I was with you in weakness and in much fear and trembling; and my speech and my message were not in plausible words of wisdom, but in demonstration of the Spirit and of power, that your faith might not rest in the wisdom of men but in the power of God. (1 Cor 2:1–5)

Because the immediate context of this passage is critical in understanding what Paul is saying, following is a brief summary. Paul is addressing the issue of division in the community in which many were aligning themselves with a particular apostle or minister. Some Christians were judging and comparing their ministers according to the values of their culture: rhetorical excellence and human wisdom. Taking their eyes off the mystery of Christ crucified, the Corinthians were ascribing their faith to qualities of the preachers themselves.[3] Paul uses this occasion to contrast human wisdom and rhetoric with the wisdom of the cross: "For Christ did not send me to baptize but to preach the gospel and not with eloquent wisdom, lest the cross of Christ be emptied of its power. For the word of the cross is folly to those who are perishing, but to us who are being saved it is the power of God" (1 Cor 1:17–18).

Paul holds the power of the cross in such high esteem in comparison to human wisdom that he seems to say that eloquent words of human wisdom can actually empty the cross of its power. According to Montague, "Paul's meaning [here] is that rhetoric is hollow, but the cross of Christ is not, nor does its power come from eloquence."[4] Only the word of the cross has power to change lives and to save; the human eloquence or wisdom of a particu-

---

3. Matera, *New Testament Theology*, 118.

4. Montague, *First Corinthians*, 41.

lar preacher is powerless without it. Paul is, therefore, not afraid to boast of his weakness in speaking—a weakness Paul knew they were aware of (2 Cor 6:5)—because he knows that it was by the power of the cross of Christ that they were converted. This leads Paul to explain the distinction between the wisdom of God manifested in the cross and the wisdom of man (1 Cor 1:18–2:16). Christ crucified is the wisdom of God, a wisdom that becomes a scandal to the Jews and foolishness to the Greeks (1 Cor 1:23–24). But, paradoxically, this wisdom of God has the power to save. Paul's emphasis on the cross allows him to highlight the power of God who manifests himself in his human weakness. Because God is manifest in human weakness, no man can boast in the presence of God (1 Cor 1:26–30). Paul, therefore, can boast in his lack of eloquence and his weaknesses, not only so that God will receive the glory for the growth they experienced through the different ministers (1 Cor 3:7), but also so that the Corinthians will see the power of the cross which defies human wisdom.[5]

This context is important as we consider the power of the gospel that was manifested in the weakness of Paul.[6] Essentially, the persuasive power of the gospel according to Paul is not a function of his personal eloquence or strength of philosophical argument but of the *message* itself, which came to them in demonstration and in power. Paul says, "My speech and my message [κήρυγμά] were not in plausible words of wisdom, but in demonstration of the Spirit and of power [ἀποδείξει πνεύματος καὶ δυνάμεως], that your faith might not rest in the wisdom of men but in the power of God" (1 Cor 2:4–5). Paul is contrasting not only the *content* of the message but also the *means by which this message persuades*;

---

5. In 2 Corinthians, Paul develops further the idea that God's power is made known in and through human weakness (2 Cor 4:7; 6:7; 12:9–10).

6. George Montague says that Paul intentionally depicts himself as weak in comparison to other great speakers. "Instead of posing with great self-confidence as a powerful speaker was expected to do, Paul was overwhelmed by his own human weakness in the face of the awesome divine message confided to him, like the "fear and trembling" with which he tell us we should work out our salvation" (Phil 2:12–13). Montague, *1 Corinthians*, 58.

it persuades not through an eloquent philosophical argument but through the "demonstration of the Spirit and of power."

According to Peter Williamson and Mary Healy, the phrase ἀποδείξει πνεύματος καὶ δυνάμεως here is best understood as a "proof" of the Spirit:

> The word 'demonstration,' *apodeixis*, means a "showing forth" or "proof." The two words 'Spirit and power' function together to refer to one reality (a figure of speech known as a *hendiadys*), the power of the Holy Spirit. Paul chooses to rely on the proof of the Spirit's power rather than clever philosophical arguments or eloquent oratory for an important reason: "so that your faith might rest not on human wisdom but on the power of God.[7]

The power of the Spirit that accompanied Paul's message offers "proof" or a "showing forth" of the message of the cross. In other words, the message of the cross is persuasive *because* it is followed by, or accompanied with, a kind of Spirit-empowered "proof."

There are, according to George Montague, several options as to what exactly Paul means by this "proof" in the Spirit and in power:

> This may refer to the miracles worked by Paul at Corinth (cf. 2 Cor 12:12), but most probably it refers to the manifest action of the Holy Spirit in both preacher and hearer, which resulted in the abundant conversions that followed his preaching, and also the charisms with which the Spirit filled the Community.[8]

Therefore, the demonstration or "proof" of the Spirit might refer to one or more of the following:

1. miracles (including healings)

2. manifest action of the Spirit in the preacher and hearers

---

7. Healy and Williamson, "Biblical Orientations for the New Evangelization," 113.

8. Montague, *First Corinthians*, 58.

3. charisms of the Spirit that filled the community.

David Garland seems to hold to number two, to the exclusion of one and three. "But in this case the proof did not come from rhetorical persuasion, it came from God. Faith is based not on how entertaining, informative, or compelling the speaker is but on the power of God transforming the hearts of hearers."[9] Here the power of the Spirit is primarily what changes the hearts of those who hear the message. Put another way, Garland says, "What is clear is that Paul attributes the Corinthians' conversion to the powerful intervention of the Spirit. He understands God's power, then, to supplant the preacher's weakness."[10] Thus, according to Garland, the "demonstration of the Spirit and power" consists in the Spirit's action *in the hearts of the hearers,* an action which supplants the preacher's weakness and gives the message its persuasive power.[11]

The most convincing interpretation, however, comes from Gordon Fee who says that the Greek word ἀπόδειξις is best understood in terms of all three: (1) miracles, signs, and wonders, (2) the action of the Spirit in the preacher and the hearers, and (3) the charisms manifested in the community. Regarding the first two, Fee maintains that Paul "frequently refers to his own effective ministry as a direct result of the work of the Spirit. This work included not only conviction concerning the truth of the gospel, but also signs and wonders, all of which resulted in changed lives."[12] Paul is, therefore, at least implying that the "proof" of the gospel

9. Garland, *1 Corinthians,* 87.

10. Ibid., 87.

11. So much is Garland convinced of this reading that he holds that the phrase "demonstration of the Spirit and in power" *cannot* refer to miracles or to divine actions in the Corinthian community. He says, "Paul is not talking about "deeds of power" (12:28) or "signs and wonders" attending his preaching (Rom 15:19; 2 Cor 12:12), but their conversion. Were he referring to miracles, he would have used the plural" (Ibid., 87). In other words, because *apodeixis* is singular and not plural, it cannot refer to the deeds of power and signs and wonders attending Paul's preaching. Garland holds that the Spirit's power at work in Paul's proclamation of the cross is the supernatural power at work in the hearts of the believers.

12. Fee, *God's Empowering Presence,* 848.

in 1 Corinthians 2:1–5 consists of the powerful conviction of the Holy Spirit and powerful signs and wonders that accompany the message.

George Montague offers an additional reason to interpret ἀπόδειξις here in terms deeds of power such as signs, wonders, and healings:

> In vs. 4, the Greek word *apodeixis*, here translated "demonstration" means a convincing proof. Philo (*De vita Moysis* 1, 95) uses it for proofs in signs and wonders in contrast to mere words. Such is Paul's meaning here, where the idea is identical with 1 Thess 1:5. The apostle's preaching, like that of Jesus, was not just something addressed to the mind. It was accompanied by healings and other charismatic manifestations.[13]

Just as Philo, the first-century Jewish exegete, used the same word (in the singular) to denote signs and wonders in the old covenant in contrast to mere words, Paul is using the very same word to refer to the signs and wonders that God works by the Spirit in the new covenant.

To bolster his conclusion, Fee ultimately employs a canonical hermeneutic by setting 1 Corinthians 2:1–5 in relation to other Pauline texts regarding Paul's Spirit-empowered proclamation in 1 Thessalonians 1:5–6 and Romans 15:18–19.[14] It is worth quoting Fee at length:

13. Montague, *The Holy Spirit*,135.

14. In 1 Thessalonians 1:5–6, Paul gives us another instance of the gospel coming in the *power* of the Spirit: "For we know, brethren beloved of God, that he has chosen you; for our gospel came to you not only in word, but also in power and in the Holy Spirit and with full conviction." While scholars generally believe that Paul is speaking here about the power of the Spirit in terms of internal conviction of the hearts of the hearers, there are scholars who understand this passage in terms of miraculous activity. Francis Martin believes "power" in 1 Thessalonians 1:5 most likely refers to "extraordinary manifestations of the Spirit: miracles, healings, exorcisms, and so forth." Martin, "The Spirit of the Lord is Upon Me," 70. Graham Twelftree also believes Paul intends miracles in 1 Thessalonians 1:5. "Paul's description of the full or unimpaired coming of the gospel in terms of not only word but also of power (cf. Rom 1:16), Holy Spirit and completeness [in 1 Thess 5:6] meant that he

These passages, and the next, make it abundantly clear that Paul understood Christian conversion to begin with Spirit-empowered proclamation, which by the same Spirit found its lodging in the heart of the hearer so as to bring conviction—of sin, as well as of the truth of the Gospel. But the Spirit's role in Paul's preaching was not limited to an "anointing" of Paul's own words, thus carrying conviction as to the truth of the gospel itself. In Rom 15:18–19 he insists that his preaching . . . was an effective combination of "word and deed," both of which were the work of the power of the Spirit . . . For Paul this double display of power (empowered words and powerful deeds) appears as presupposition to his understanding of the role of the eschatological Spirit.[15]

If this "double display of power" becomes the "proof" of the gospel for Paul in his other letters, then it is likely that Paul is referring to miracles when he speaks of demonstration in 1 Corinthians 2:1–5.[16] This conclusion is reinforced by the fact that, according to 2 Corinthians 12:12, the Corinthians may have already known Paul to be a worker of miracles: "The signs of a true apostle were performed among you in all patience, with signs and wonders and

---

understood the gospel came not only in his preaching: the gospel came in the words he conveyed to his listeners and also—simultaneously, we probably are to assume—in the miraculous expressions of the Spirit. These went beyond the miracles such as healing and exorcism, for example, to include the breadth and the unimpaired entirety of the miraculous as Paul understood it." Twelftree, *Paul and the Miraculous,* 186–87.

15. Fee, *God's Empowering Presence,* 849.

16. Graham Twelftree agrees. "In Greek rhetoric an *apodeixis* was a technical word for a compelling conclusion to be drawn from a reasoned argument (e.g., Plato *Tim.* 40E; 4 Macc 3:19). However, the compelling proof of Paul's message was not in his rhetoric but in the demonstrations "of Spirit and of power" (1 Cor 2:4). As 'Spirit' and 'power' can be interchangeable in Paul's writing (cf. Rom 15:13, 19; 1 Thess 1:5), both words here are likely to signify the same reality. In contrasting his weakness, fear and spoken word with the demonstration of the gospel, Paul is probably referring not only to the Corinthians' encounter with God's power to transform their lives in conversion, including the reception of the Spirit accompanied by spirit gifts, but also to the miracles involved in his mission as the demonstration or proof of his gospel." Twelftree, "Signs, Wonders, Miracles," 876.

mighty works."[17] Paul apparently thought that these signs, wonders, and miracles were so constitutive of his apostolic ministry of preaching that they served as authentic signs of his authority as an apostle. Moreover, Paul's appeal to the various signs of his apostleship implies that the Corinthians experienced or witnessed these miracles as he preached the gospel to them.[18] Thus the "double display of power" in Spirit-empowered words and deeds, which include healing, is the most fitting interpretation of ἀπόδειξις.

Thus, read in light of other Pauline passages, the phrase "in demonstration of Spirit and of power" in 1 Corinthians 2:4 refers to the supernatural *proof* that accompanied Paul's message of the cross that led to the conversion of the Corinthians. This proof of the Spirit at least includes (1) the Spirit's action in the anointed preacher and the hearer, and (2) supernatural deeds such as miracles, signs, wonders, and healings. If this reading is correct, Paul is essentially telling the Corinthians that their faith does not rest on the skill of a particular preacher, but rather on the message of Christ crucified that is proven to them by the power of the Spirit in signs, wonders, and healings.[19]

17. According to Max Turner, "healings of various kinds would almost certainly be the *main* (though by no means exclusive) content of the language of 'signs and wonders' [in Paul]." Turner, *The Holy Spirit and Spiritual Gifts,* 247.

18. It is significant that references to miracles in Paul's writings only occur in the letters to the churches where his apostleship and credentials are under question. For example, in Paul's earlier letters (1 Thessalonians, Philippians, and Philemon) where Paul is not defending or seeking to introduce himself as an apostle, there are no clear references to miracles. But in Romans, 1 and 2 Corinthians, and Galatians, where there are clear references to miracles, we find Paul asserting and/or defending his apostolic authority to preach the gospel. Twelftree, *Paul and the Miraculous,* 224–25.

19. As opposed to his earlier article where his conclusion is much broader, Twelftree argues in his later comprehensive study that *apodeixis* refers *only* to the miracles that accompanied the gospel. "As a demonstration or proof that came with Paul's proclamation, 'of Spirit and of power' was neither a power inherent in the message nor any response by the Corinthians; rather, the phrase refers to the miraculous expression of the message of the power of God." Twelftree, *Paul and the Miraculous,* 200.

In 1 Corinthians 2:1–5, Paul, therefore, articulates a link between the preaching of the gospel and deeds of healing. These deeds accompany the preaching of the gospel and serve as a kind of *convincing proof* of the truth of the gospel of Christ that stands in marked contrast to the philosophical proof of a polished preacher. What makes the gospel persuasive is not just the content of the message, Christ crucified, but the *means by which that message persuades*; that is, with a *demonstration* of the Spirit's power. Significantly, this Spirit-empowered demonstration of the content of the message is for Paul the foundation of the faith engendered by its proclamation (1 Cor 2:5). Otherwise, the faith would be subject to the weak foundation of man's wisdom. For Paul, it is both the message (word) and its supernatural demonstration (deed) that forms the foundation of faith.[20]

The next text of Paul where we discover the confluence of the preaching of the gospel and the power of the Spirit is in his letter to the Galatians:

> Let me ask you only this: Did you receive the Spirit by works of the law, or by hearing with faith? Having begun with the Spirit, are you now ending with the flesh? Did you experience so many things in vain?—if it really is in vain. Does he who supplies the Spirit to you and works miracles among you do so by works of the law, or by hearing with faith? (Gal 3:2–5)

In the context of his letter to the Galatians, Paul is defending his ministry against the Judaizers who had come to Galatia after Paul preached there. These false apostles were teaching that the Galatians needed to live like Jews and thus not only needed to be circumcised but also needed to follow the entire Law or risk losing their salvation.[21] Paul, therefore, responds by teaching strongly that the Galatians are justified before God through faith in Christ

---

20. According to Greig, "Paul teaches that *both* the object of one's faith—Christ, the message of the Truth—*and* God demonstrating the truth by His power in our lives strengthen and reinforce our faith." Greig, *The Kingdom and the Power*, 150.

21. Gorman, *Apostle of the Crucified Lord*, 189.

and not by the works of the law. Thus, in chapters 1 and 2 Paul defends his apostolic authority and teaches emphatically that since it is by faith in Christ that men are justified before God, the works of the law are powerless and should be rejected lest men lose their share in Christ.

After using the provocative language of a rebuke, Paul in chapter 3 employs a series of rhetorical questions about the Galatians' initial experience of the Spirit when they came to faith as part of his argument regarding the powerlessness of the works of the law. "Did you receive the Spirit by works of the law, or by hearing with faith? Having begun with the Spirit, are you now ending with the flesh?" (3:2–3). Paul intentionally highlights the reception of the Spirit that came through hearing with faith in their initial conversion because it corroborates the truth of his theology.[22] This leads Paul to ask: "Did you experience so many things in vain— if it really is in vain?" (3:4). This line implies two things: (1) the Galatians' own experience of the Spirit proves that the Judaizers are theologically wrong about the works of the law, and (2) if the Galatians revert to doing the works of the law they will lose their life in Christ.[23]

This context leads us to the verse that concerns us. Paul again appeals to the Galatians' experience of faith as a kind of argument: "Does he who supplies the Spirit to you and works miracles among you [ἐνεργῶν δυνάμεις ἐν ὑμῖν] do so by works of the law, or by hearing with faith?" (3:5)[24] Two relevant points can be drawn out

22. Paul's argument from experience complements his theological argumentation in chapter 2. Fee, *God's Empowering Presence*, 382.

23. Some scholars believe that since the Greek word for experience (ἐπάθετε) in verse 4 can also be translated as "to suffer," Paul is not primarily speaking about the experience of the Spirit in their initial conversion to faith but the sufferings they experienced on account of that faith. Gorman, *Apostle of the Crucified Lord*, 191–92. Regardless of whether this is the case, the following verse (v. 5) shows the clear connection between the Spirit's action in miracles and initial conversion.

24. It is implausible to interpret ἐνεργῶν δυνάμεις as anything other than the "workings of miracles" that include healings. For a thorough demonstration that δυνάμεις is translated in the New Testament as miracles that include healing, see Grundmann, "δύναμαι," 284–317.

of Paul's final rhetorical question. First, if Paul uses the initial manifest presence of the Spirit in workings of miracles among them as *evidence* in an argument about the superiority of "hearing with faith," then we can at least affirm the *presence* of these miracles in his initial proclamation of the gospel.[25] Paul's argument only makes sense if workings of miracles actually accompanied his preaching of the gospel to the Galatians.[26] Second, the weight of Paul's argument is that the presence of miracles in the preaching of the gospel—both in the initial proclamation and in the present experience of the community—serves as a kind of proof of the veracity of that gospel over and against the powerlessness of the works of the law.[27]

Therefore, in Gal 3:2–5 we have evidence that (1) miracles of healing in fact accompanied Paul's initial preaching of the gospel to the Galatians (i.e., when they heard with faith), and (2) the presence of these miracles is used by Paul as proof that faith in Christ, by which these miracles were done, is true.

The final Pauline text to consider in which we discover a link between the proclamation of the gospel and healing is Romans 15:18–19:

> For I will not venture to speak of anything except what Christ has wrought through me to win obedience from the Gentiles, by word and deed, by the power of signs and wonders, by the power of the Holy Spirit, so that from Jerusalem and as far round as Illyricum I have fully preached the gospel of Christ.

25. Since the two participles, "who supplies the Spirit and works miracles" go together here, we can conclude that Paul is claiming that the reception of the Spirit also includes "various expressions of the Spirit" including the working of miracles. Fee, *Empowering Presence*, 388.

26. Tarazi, *Galatians*, 106.

27. The present tense of the Greek verbs "he who supplies (ἐπιχορηγῶν) the Spirit and works (ἐνεργῶν) miracles" in verse 5 indicates that these miracles were ongoing and present in the Galatian church. This demonstrates that miracles perform a greater function than confirming the truth of the gospel in its initial proclamation; they manifest the character of God who continually does such things (Jer 10:12; 51:15; Dan 2:20). Bruce, *The Epistle to the Galatians*, 151; and Hansen, *Galatians*, 82–83.

In the context of our passage (15:7–15) Paul reminds the Romans that he is bold in his writing to them because, by the grace of Christ, he has become a minister to the Gentiles who according to the prophets are destined to glorify God for his mercy. Paul understands his mission to minister in the "priestly service of the gospel of God, so that the offering of the Gentiles may be acceptable, sanctified by the Holy Spirit" (v. 16), a ministry that leads him to boast of his work in Christ Jesus (v. 17). Confident that Jesus has made him a minister of the gospel to the Gentiles, Paul explains his boasting in the next sentence. "I will not venture [τολμάω] to speak of anything except what Christ has wrought [κατειργάσατο] through me to win obedience from the Gentiles" (v. 17).[28]

Given that Paul understands his mission to the Gentiles in terms of bringing about their "obedience of faith" (Rom 1:6; 16:26), he does not dare to speak of anything except of what Christ did to accomplish that mission. How did Christ accomplish this mission through Paul? The answer follows: "by word and deed, by the power of signs and wonders, by the power of the Holy Spirit [λόγῳ καὶ ἔργῳ, ἐν δυνάμει σημείων καὶ τεράτων, ἐν δυνάμει πνεύματος]" (v. 18). The obedience of faith of the Gentiles was accomplished by Christ through Paul in a gospel of word and deed. The deeds, as Paul explains, consisted of signs, wonders, and healings all done by the power of the Holy Spirit. Twelftree believes this phrase means that Paul's preaching arose out of the healings and miracles done in the Spirit just as in the ministry of Jesus.[29]

Robert Jewett argues that the double reference to God's "power" is significant because it reflects the miracles occurring in the Christian community in Rome, while also indicating how miracles functioned in Christ's work through Paul.[30]

---

28. The word τολμάω can be more literally translated "to dare." It is the same word the evangelists used when describing people who did not "dare" to ask Jesus any more questions. The word κατειργάσατο, here translated as "wrought," can also be translated as "accomplished."

29. Twelftree, *Paul and the Miraculous*, 222.

30. Jewett, *Romans*, 911.

The "matter of fact" character of this double reference to divine δύναμις is quite striking, particularly in a letter addressed to the center of the Roman imperium, and it is clear that both Paul and his audience in Rome assume that such manifestations of miracle-working power are routine features in every authentic house and tenement church. They are signs that Christ is present and active in the new, eschatological community (15:17–18) evoking "obedience" to the gospel (15:18), setting relationships right, and thereby producing social "holiness" (15:16). Insofar as they demonstrate the power of Paul's regent, these signs authenticate his ambassadorial role, and the appropriateness of his addressing the varied Christian communities in Rome.[31]

In this way, the power of the Spirit that produces the signs of Christ's presence accomplishes Christ's work and simultaneously authenticates Paul's role as an ambassador of Christ to the Christians in Rome.

Furthermore, according to Jewett, the word ὥστε of the next phrase of our text designates the *result* of the deeds of power that accompanied Paul's preaching which achieved the obedience of the Gentiles:[32] " . . . so that [ὥστε] from Jerusalem and as far round as Illyricum I have fully preached the gospel of Christ, thus making it my ambition to preach the gospel" (15:19–20). Some scholars believe that Paul, in this subordinate clause, casts his entire ministry in terms of the signs and wonders that brought the Gentiles to the obedience of faith. Twelftree explains:

> Paul does not see his ministry of proclaiming the gospel as confined to, or understood only in terms of, his words or the verbal message he preaches. Indeed, in the final clause where he describes the result of his ministry—so that [ὥστε] from Jerusalem and as far around as

31. Ibid., 911.

32. Ibid., 911. Jewett believes it is incorrect to translate ὥστε as the beginning of another sentence. Rather, ὥστε is operating as a dependent clause reaching back to include the material from verse 17 onwards, thus explaining the scope of Paul's mission to the Gentiles in verse 16.

Illyricum I have fulfilled [πεπληρωκέναι] the gospel of Christ' (Rom 15:19b)—he allows word and deed, signs and wonders to stand for his entire ministry. For Paul, therefore (fulfilling or proclaiming) the gospel involves not only words or propositions, but also actions or deeds empowered by the Spirit, in particular miracles.[33]

This suggests, therefore, that the Spirit-empowered signs, wonders, and healings that accompany Paul's ministry of preaching to the Gentiles were not an occasional aspect of his ministry but happened wherever he preached.[34]

If this reading of Romans 15:17–19 is correct, then we can conclude that not only did Paul's preaching to the Gentiles have two components (words and deeds), but also that this two-part gospel is what characterized his ministry everywhere. It was this two-part gospel of Paul that had the effect of achieving the obedience of faith among Gentile unbelievers.[35] From this passage it is likely that, according to Paul, the deeds of power (including healings) that accompany the preaching of the gospel cannot be reduced to rare and extrinsic proofs of the gospel; rather, they constitute an expected and intrinsic expression of it.[36]

33. Twelftree, *Paul and the Miraculous*, 223.

34. Ibid., 223.

35. Frank Matera describes it this way: "It is an obedience that came about as the result of God's powerful work, which has been manifested in 'word and deed' (the proclamation of the gospel and the effect of that gospel on the lives of those who have embraced it) and 'the power of signs and wonders' (the signs pointing to God's work and the wonders leading people to praise God). The power behind all of this, however, is not Paul's own power but the power of God's Spirit." Matera, *Romans*, 333.

36. Paul understands the miraculous as *integral* to his preaching of the gospel. Twelftree argues: "We cannot avoid concluding that Paul did not consider his gospel to be merely preaching. Nor were the miracles secondary to the preaching. Instead, the gospel was always word and deed: a message of salvation realized and (therefore) authenticated by the Spirit's manifestation or materialization in the miraculous." Twelftree, *Paul and the Miraculous*, 225.

The Charism of Healing

In his first letter to the Corinthians, Paul discusses a selection of charisms or gifts of the Spirit and mentions healing three times (1 Cor 12:9, 28, 30). That Paul names the charism of healing as active in the Corinthian community is remarkable in its own right. The precise connection, however, between the charism of healing and the proclamation of the gospel is admittedly difficult to discern, since Paul's teaching on charisms concerns their proper place among other charisms, and not necessarily their purpose for evangelization. Nevertheless, this difficulty does not render our study fruitless. The connection between healing and the proclamation of the gospel will become clearer as we consider both the presence of the charism of healing in the Corinthian community in terms of how healing appears in the New Testament as a whole, and the relationship between the charism of healing and Paul's exhortation to the Corinthians to "earnestly desire the higher gifts" to build up the body of Christ.

The most extensive treatment of the charisms of the Spirit is found in 1 Corinthians 12–14, where Paul addresses the topic of charisms in terms of the unity and diversity of the body of Christ.[37] There is general agreement among scholars that the problem Paul addresses in 1 Corinthians 12–14 is the overemphasis on the gift of tongues in the Corinthian community.[38] To the Corinthians,

---

37. The Greek word *charisma* occurs seventeen times in the New Testament and is used in various ways. The word can denote the "free gift" of salvation (Rom 6:23) or more specifically the gift of a "state of life" such as virginity in 1 Corinthians 7:7 or other "gifts" of the Spirit (1 Tim 4:14 and 2 Tim 1:6). Most of the references to charisms in the New Testament, however, employ the term in a more technical sense as "gifts" of the Spirit. These charisms cannot be reduced to natural talents or acquired skills. Rather, charisms are "supernatural gifts that either enable what is humanly impossible (such as healing or miracles) or enhance a natural gift, such as teaching or service, to a level of supernatural efficacy . . . Charisms are distinct from sanctifying grace given at baptism, in that they are given not primarily for the personal sanctification of the recipient but to be exercised for the good of others." Doctrinal Commission of the ICCRS, *Baptism in the Holy Spirit*, 45-46.

38. Perhaps it is more accurate to say an *incorrect* emphasis on the gift of tongues. Njiru, *Charisms and the Holy Spirit's Activity in the Body of Christ*,

the gift of tongues was the most esteemed of all the gifts, likely because it seemed to be the most noticeably *spiritual* of all of the manifestations of the Spirit in the community. This false emphasis led to divisions in the community and disorder in public worship, as Paul addresses in 1 Corinthians 13–14.[39] Paul's reflections in 1 Corinthians 12–14, therefore, have a double purpose: to situate the gift of tongues and prophecy among the other charisms of the Spirit in the church, and to resolve the pastoral problem caused by the misplaced emphasis on this gift in community worship.[40]

Paul begins his response by offering a varied but not exhaustive list of gifts or charisms given to the community:

> Now there are varieties of gifts [χαρισμάτων], but the same Spirit; and there are varieties of service, but the same Lord; and there are varieties of working, but it is the same God who inspires them all in every one. To each is given the manifestation of the Spirit for the common good. To one is given through the Spirit the utterance of wisdom, and to another the utterance of knowledge according to the same Spirit, to another faith by the same Spirit, to another gifts of healing by the one Spirit, to another prophecy, to another the ability to distinguish between spirits, to another various kinds of tongues, to another the interpretation of tongues. All these are inspired by one and the same Spirit, who apportions to each one individually as he wills. (1 Cor 12:7–12)

Emphasizing the diversity of charisms given by the one Spirit, Paul essentially makes charisms the principle of differentiation of function in the body of Christ. Thus, the diversity of the body of Christ is identified with the diversity of the charisms of the Spirit.[41] According to Paul's image of the church as a body with vari-

---

44–45.

39. Sullivan, *Charisms and Charismatic Renewal*, 20–21.

40. Njiru, *Charisms and the Holy Spirit's Activity in the Body of Christ*, 45.

41. Sullivan, *Charisms and Charismatic Renewal*, 19. "It is charisms that determine which function each member of the body is to have, and that enable each member to perform that function. Thus for Paul charisms are essential

ous parts, no member of the body enjoys the operation of all of the charisms of the Spirit.[42] Moreover, Paul's description implies that the charisms listed, including "gifts of healing," are in fact operative in the community. The presence of the "gifts of healing" (χαρίσματα ἰαμάτων) in the community for Paul is not an exception but a normative element of the church's life.[43] The presence of "gifts of healing" in the community is confirmed later in 12:28:

> Now you are the body of Christ and individually members of it. And God has appointed in the church first apostles, second prophets, third teachers, then workers of miracles, then healers [χαρίσματα ἰαμάτων], helpers, administrators, speakers in various kinds of tongues.

The gift of healing must have been present enough in the Corinthian community to warrant Paul mentioning it multiple times in his discussion of the place of charisms in the body of Christ.

To translate the phrase χαρίσματα ἰαμάτων as "healers" is a little misleading. Since the phrase χαρίσματα ἰαμάτων in verses 8, 28, and 30 is a genitive plural construction, it is better translated "gifts of healings" or "gifts which result in healings."[44] These gifts, according to Albert Vanhoye, do not refer to the healings themselves but the grace given to certain members of the body who in fact are used to heal others.[45] Scholars are divided as to whether

---

to the very structure of the Christian community . . . There is no doubt that for Paul a Christian community without a variety of charisms operative in its members would be unthinkable; it would no longer be like a living body, and hence no longer 'a body of Christ.'" Ibid., 19.

42. By discussing charisms in terms of a body, Paul neutralizes the Corinthian hyper-emphasis on the gift of tongues and places them in the context of other gifts of the Spirit present in the community.

43. Paul seems to imply that the Corinthian community was fully endowed with every charism in 1 Corinthians 1:7, where he thanks God for the grace given to the Corinthians who were not "lacking in any spiritual gift [χαρίσματι]."

44. Sullivan, *Charisms and Charismatic Renewal*, 157.

45. Vanhoye, *I Carismi nel Nuovo Testamenti*, 101. "Tuttavia l'unione del plural di guarigioni con il singolare della persona ("a un altro") mostra che non si tratta di una persona che ottiene la guarigione per se stessa, bensì di una che ottiene guarigioni per altre. Non e un potere suo, ma sempre una grazia che

or not the plural construction here indicates a stable gift of healing in a particular person or more precisely that certain people receive a unique gift of healing each time they are used to heal.[46] Regardless, Catholic teaching confirms that while God can grant healing through the individual prayer of any Christian, there are those who, in fact, have a charism of healing in that they are used with more frequency in the healing of others.[47]

If the phrase "gifts of healings" in verses 8, 28, and 30 refers to particular gifted members of the body used to bring healing to others, then it is reasonable to conclude, given our study thus far, that those endowed with this gift likely included those preaching the gospel. In fact, when the charism of healing is defined more broadly as any healing that occurs as a response to prayer, then we can, as Sullivan does, understand the healings of the New Testament as examples of the charism of healing in action. If this is true, then the healings in Jesus' ministry, in Acts, and in Paul's letters are, broadly speaking, concrete instances of the charism of healing at work.[48] Given the close relationship between evangelization and healing we have seen throughout the New Testament, it would be very likely that those in the community with the "charisms of healings" would include those who preach the gospel.[49] We can conclude that one reason, if not the main one, the Spirit grants

---

dipende ogni volta dal beneplacito di Dio." Ibid., 101.

46. Fee, *God's Empowering Presence,* 169. According to Njiru, "The fact that χαρίσματα ἰαμάτων are given to some Christians suggests that some members in the community are used as channels or instruments of the divine power to heal." Njiru, *Charisms and the Holy Spirit's Activity,* 153.

47. *Catechism of the Catholic Church,* sec 1508; Doctrinal Commission of the ICCRS, *Guidelines on Prayers,* 41.

48. Sullivan, *Charisms and Charismatic Renewal,* 165.

49. There is a tension, but no contradiction, between Jesus' universal command to heal the sick, the commissioning accounts, and the fact that there are particular people gifted with the charism of healing the sick as we see in 1 Corinthians 12. Given the pronounced role healing plays in evangelization in the New Testament, the charism of healing must be related to evangelization. To make sense of the New Testament data, it is reasonable to conclude that either the evangelists themselves had the charism of healing or those with the charism were present as the gospel was preached.

"charisms of healings" to the church is for the effective proclamation the gospel.

When Paul asks the Corinthians a series of rhetorical questions regarding the complementarity of the spiritual gifts, questions that have the expected answer of "no" (vv. 29–31), he adds an exhortation that is relevant to the relationship between the charism of healing and the preaching of the gospel. "Are all apostles? Are all prophets? Are all teachers? Do all work miracles? Do all possess gifts of healing? Do all speak with tongues? Do all interpret? But earnestly desire the higher gifts. And I will show you a still more excellent way" (1 Cor 12:29–31). While these questions imply *de facto* that there were some in the community who had "gifts of healing" and others who did not, Paul nevertheless exhorts the Corinthians to "earnestly desire the higher gifts" (12:31). Even later, after his discussion of love, he adds: "make love your aim and earnestly desire the spiritual gifts, especially that you may prophesy" (14:1).[50] Paul's double exhortation to the Corinthians to "earnestly desire" the spiritual gifts is significant as we consider healing and evangelization.

According to Paul, the charisms of the Spirit are primarily given for the purpose of building up the body of Christ.[51] This building up of the body by means of the charisms is ultimately the reason Paul begins to discuss in the next chapter the *purpose of charisms*: love. Without love, the charisms have no value or purpose.[52] For Paul, therefore, when charisms are rightly ordered they are not opposed to love; they are rather *expressions and tools of love* which build up the body of Christ in the one Spirit. Paul's

50. Paul's exhortation to seek the gift of prophecy, a gift that Paul deems higher than that of tongues, indicates the value Paul places on a gift's ability to build up the body of Christ (1 Cor 14).

51. The purpose of the charisms is laid out in several places in 1 Corinthians. In 12:7 Paul says: "To each is given the manifestation of the Spirit for the *common good* [πρὸς τὸ συμφέρον]." Paul is even more explicit that the charisms are for the "building up" of the church as we see in 14:5, 12, and 26. See Njiru, *The Holy Spirit's Activity*, 129, 195; and Sullivan, *Charisms and Charismatic Renewal*, 30.

52. Njiru, *The Holy Spirit's Activity*, 60.

exhortation to make love the aim and seek the higher gifts is thus an exhortation to build up the community in love by means of the charisms. Given the ability of charisms to build up the body of Christ, it seems that Paul does not want the Corinthians to be satisfied with the charisms they currently exercise but to continue to be zealous in seeking greater ones.[53]

Interestingly, Paul's exhortation to seek the charisms presupposes that the Corinthians are, in fact, able to receive more charisms of the Spirit than what they are currently manifesting in their lives. Put another way, Paul's double exhortation assumes that it is possible to seek and receive charisms, charisms that one is not currently manifesting for the purpose of building up the body of Christ. This seems to apply to all of the gifts, especially those related to preaching the gospel.[54] Since the charism of healing plays a significant role in the preaching of the gospel and thus the growth of the church in the New Testament, Paul's double exhortation suggests that the members of the church who evangelize can (and perhaps should) implore the Spirit in faith for an increase of the charism of healing for a more effective evangelization.[55]

53. The Greek word for "earnestly desire" (ζηλοῦτε) in 12:31 and 14:1 is in the present tense and is the same word from which we get the English word zealous. Thus, a more literal English translation could read: "Continue to be zealous in seeking the higher gifts."

54. Even outside the explicit proclamation of the gospel, the presence of miracles and healings in the Corinthian community must have had an effect on unbelievers outside the community. Robert Plummer explains, "When Paul says all gifts (including miracles) should be used for 'building up' (*oikodome*) the church, this building up includes both the incorporation of new believers as well as the maturing of present ones (14:23–26). Non-believers will be attracted and converted through the miracles performed by gifted members of the Corinthian church. Indeed, if one of the main purposes of the apostles' miracles is to confirm the gospel message, it would be surprising if miracles performed by non-apostles did not serve a similar function." Plummer, *Paul's Understanding of the Church's Mission*, 109–10.

55. A concrete scriptural example of the early church earnestly seeking the higher gifts can be found in Acts 4, where the apostolic church implores the Spirit to grant them boldness in preaching and signs, wonders, and healings. The disciples, having already received the fullness of the Spirit in Acts 2, received an additional outpouring of the Spirit by which they received an

Summary and Conclusion

Having examined several passages of Paul in part one of this chapter, we can draw two similar conclusions about the relationship between the preaching of the gospel and physical healing. First, *for Paul the proclamation of the gospel does not come without deeds of power by which the Spirit provides proof of the gospel's authenticity.* In his letter to the Corinthians, Paul makes clear that his initial proclamation of the message of the gospel (Christ crucified) came to them with a "demonstration of Spirit and power" that not only included the supernatural conviction of the Holy Spirit in the heart of the preacher and the listeners, but also miracles and healings. In downplaying the role of eloquence, rhetoric, and worldly wisdom in his preaching, Paul maintains that the faith of the Corinthians rests not merely on the content of his message but on the *proof* that accompanied the message. Taking into account similar passages of Paul, we can conclude that deeds of healing play an irreplaceable role in proving Paul's message of Christ crucified. Miracles and healings were also present to such a degree in Paul's initial proclamation to the Galatians that he uses their continued presence as an argument for the truth about Christ from whom they receive the Spirit. For Paul, therefore, the healings that accompany the message of the gospel serve as a kind of proof of the authenticity of the gospel itself.[56]

Second, *the healings that accompany the gospel are not merely extrinsic demonstrations of the gospel; they are intrinsic expressions of it.* For Paul, the gospel comes in two parts: the word (message)

---

increase of charisms for the purpose of building up the body of Christ in evangelization. They asked in faith and they received.

56. We find a similarly strong conclusion in the Letter to the Hebrews. "[The gospel] was declared at first by the Lord, and it was attested to us by those who heard him, while God also bore witness by *signs and wonders and various miracles and by gifts of the Holy Spirit* distributed according to his own will" (Heb 2:3b–4, emphasis mine). Significantly, the author of Hebrews combines signs, wonders, and gifts of the Holy Spirit as the way God bears witness to the authenticity of the gospel. While Pauline authorship of Hebrews is doubtful, this passage is thoroughly Pauline because it confirms his understanding of the role healing plays in the preaching of the gospel.

and the deeds (of power) that accompany it. The two-part gospel is most notably evident in Paul's description of achieving the obedience of the Gentiles in Romans 15, where he speaks about his gospel coming in both word and deed. Miracles of healing do not just authenticate the gospel; they manifest the presence of Jesus who is preached and thus are an expression of the gospel.[57] Therefore, the miracles and healings that accompany the preaching of the gospel cannot be reduced to rare and extrinsic proofs of the gospel but remain, according to Paul, an expected and intrinsic expression of it.[58]

From the presence of "charisms of healings" in the Corinthian community we can draw two conclusions regarding the relationship between healing and the preaching of the gospel. First, *Paul's description of the body of Christ suggests that there are indeed some Christians that receive "gifts of healings" and, therefore, are used more commonly for healing than those without them.* Granting our limited understanding of how the charism is used in the community, the presence of the charism of healing in Corinth can be understood in light of the presence of the charism elsewhere in the New Testament. If we understand charisms as graces given by the Spirit for the building up of the body, then the healings we see in the proclamation of the gospel in the ministry of Jesus, the apostolic church in Acts, and in Paul are examples of the charism of healing given in the proclamation of the gospel for the sake of building up the body of Christ. In fact, as it is depicted in the New Testament, *the charism of healing is so closely linked with evangelization that the church should expect the presence of the charism in the preaching of the gospel.*

57. Twelftree, *Paul and the Miraculous*, 322; and Fee, *God's Empowering Presence*, 849.

58. Twelftree describes the intrinsic link between the two in strong language. "The gospel was a composite expression of the audible and the tangible powerful presence of God. *For Paul, no more could the gospel be proclaimed without words than it could come or be experienced without miracles. Without the miraculous, Paul may have had a message, but he would not have had a gospel. Without the miraculous, there was no gospel, only preaching.*" Twelftree, *Paul and the Miraculous*, 317.

Second, Paul's double exhortation to "earnestly desire" the spiritual gifts relates the charism of healing to evangelization. Paul's exhortation presupposes that one can "earnestly desire" charisms that one is not currently manifesting for the purpose of building up the body of Christ. In a curious tension with his own image of the body of Christ as endowed with a diversity of charisms, Paul exhorts the Corinthians not to settle with the charisms they are currently manifesting, but rather to zealously seek and receive higher charisms from the Spirit. *Given the critical role healing plays in the preaching of the gospel for Paul, those Christians who want to build up the body through evangelization can implore the Spirit for the charism of healing to accompany their preaching.* Interestingly, there is a scriptural example of this "earnestly desiring" and seeking of the charism of healing in Acts 4. Having already received the fullness of the Spirit, the apostolic church comes together in prayer and implores God for more boldness in preaching and signs, wonders, and healings to accompany their preaching. The result of the apostolic zeal in seeking from the Lord more charisms of the Spirit was an extraordinarily effective evangelization that led to the extensive growth of the body of Christ.

Chapter 4

Healing and the New Evangelization

ANY RESPONSE TO JOHN Paul II's call for a new evangelization requires an understanding of the cultural milieu in which the gospel is preached. The preaching of the gospel, if it is to be effective in the United States, must be able to illuminate the minds and capture the hearts of those steeped in the contemporary culture's philosophical worldview of postmodernism. This concluding chapter will (1) briefly outline why the gospel that is accompanied by physical healing is uniquely poised to meet the challenge of engaging the postmodern world, and (2) offer by way of conclusion four theological and pastoral considerations on how the church can move forward in integrating healing into the preaching of the gospel for an effective new evangelization.

Healing and the Challenge
of Engaging Postmodern Culture

While defining postmodern philosophy and the Western culture that has imbibed its premises is beyond the scope of this book, it is enough to describe postmodernism as the rejection and deconstruction of the modern project's attempt to understand all of reality by human reason. According to Marguerite Peeters,

> Postmodernity implies a destabilization of our rational
> or theological apprehension of reality, of the anthropo-
> logical structure given by God to man and woman, and
> the order of the universe as established by God. The ba-
> sic tenet of postmodernity is that every reality is a social
> construct, that truth and reality have no stable and ob-
> jective content—that in fact they do not exist.[1]

Permeated by postmodern assumptions, the culture of the
United States (and most of the West) is ensnared in a *perpetual
crisis of truth.* As a result, contemporary culture has four general
characteristics: (1) the loss of meta-narratives, (2) the loss of absolute truth, (3) skepticism about history, and (4) a general loss of
meaning.[2] Such a culture, on the one hand, *by default* resists the
gospel because the gospel proposes a meta-narrative of salvation
history in which the one God sends his Son to be the universal
Savior for everyone. Such absolute truth claims offend the postmodern "rights" of people to discover and determine their own
truth and meaning in life. A culture permeated by moral relativ-
ism, radical autonomy, and religious pluralism—all of which
constitute the rotten fruit of the philosophical skepticism of postmodern philosophy—is quite allergic to the absolute moral and
theological truth claims of traditional Christianity. Therefore,
an evangelization that seeks primarily to *persuade intellectually*
postmodern culture about the truth of Christianity will face significant setbacks and have little success. But, on the other hand,
if the church understands and recognizes the various features of
contemporary culture and responds accordingly, evangelization is
not only possible, but can be very fruitful.[3]

1. Peeters, *The New Global Ethic*, 13.

2. Hille, "The Uniqueness of Christ in a Postmodern World and the Challenge of World Religions," 17–29.

3. For an excellent but succinct analysis of postmodern culture and how
the Catholic Church can calibrate its evangelization efforts accordingly, see the
unpublished paper of Thomas Smith, "Postmodernism and the New Evangelization." For more theoretical works on the philosophical roots of postmodernism and how Christians can take advantage of these roots in their preaching see
James K.A. Smith, *Who's Afraid of Postmodernism?*; Chris Altrock, *Preaching to*

Because skepticism about objective truth permeates Western culture, one consequent feature of contemporary culture is the positive emphasis placed on *personal experience*.[4] Without a personal experience of an objective truth, the presentation of a particular truth is often regarded as an external imposition of another's worldview. In such a context, personal experiences carry more *epistemic authority* for the individual in both coming to know the truth and in discovering ultimate meaning. Regardless of the philosophical presuppositions of a particular culture, signs that appeal directly to one's senses and simultaneously point to transcendent truths are difficult to deny and, therefore, are very powerful in leading people to believe those truths. Tangible signs have the power to lead people to the realities to which they point. If this is true, then any tangible personal experience of the objective truths of Christianity has the power to open minds and hearts to the truth of the gospel.[5] Thus, when a person experiences God in some tangible way, for example, in the experience of physical healing, then it is more likely that person will be open to the truth proclaimed.

An evangelization that appeals to the mind with objective truths about Jesus but disregards an experiential aspect (i.e., deeds of healing) will, therefore, not be as effective with a postmodern audience as the same presentation of the gospel would be if accompanied by signs that demonstrate or express the truth of the very message that is preached.[6] Simply put, the message of the gospel accompanied by signs has more epistemic authority than a message without signs. Further, in a pluralistic society the signs of power that accompany the gospel of Jesus Christ have the net

---

Pluralists; and David Wells, *Above All Earthly Pow'rs*.

4. Hille, "The Uniqueness of Christ," 17.

5. In particular, an experience of healthy Christian community life is one of *the* most powerful ways to witness to the truth of Christianity in a fractured, postmodern world.

6. We can also argue philosophically (and theologically) that, given the nature of the human person in his body/soul composite, the proclamation of the gospel that is accompanied with signs is always more effective than a gospel without signs, no matter the culture in which a person lives.

effect of confirming the truth of the message of the gospel as opposed to the message of other religions that do not offer such demonstrative and confirmative signs. Given the crisis of truth in postmodern culture, the credibility of the gospel cannot be established by merely preaching a rationally superior vision of reality, as Christianity does indeed offer. Rather, the church's evangelization needs to highlight and invite people to a *personal experience of the gospel* to reach today's culture. One concrete and powerful way of doing this is intentionally seeking signs of healing to accompany the preaching of the gospel.

Related to the postmodern value of personal experience is the subsequent appreciation for, and credibility given to, *personal testimony*. The fragmentation of postmodern culture which is due in large part to the lack of social cohesion and common language that results from individualism, leads many people to value personal testimonies. Personal testimonies in the postmodern world are not easily dismissed because they are unique, identifiable, interesting, relevant, and personal. Therefore, testimonies carry a certain epistemic authority that arguments and critical reason do not.[7] In the postmodern world, this means that personal testimonies are a privileged way of witnessing to the objective truth about Christ. Coupled with the preaching of the truth of Jesus, the witness of those who have personally experienced an encounter with Christ and the gospel has a convincing appeal to people today. If this is true about an encounter with the love of Christ in general, then it is especially true of a testimony of someone who is physically healed as a result of such an encounter. We see this dynamic in Jesus' ministry. As Jesus manifests the inbreaking of the kingdom of God with signs, the people who testify to these signs serve the role of assisting others in opening their hearts to the truth of what he preaches. Just as personal testimonies of healings performed this role in the ministry of Jesus, a contemporary testimony of healing has the epistemic power to break people free from the narrow confines of the postmodern worldview and open them up to the God

---

7. Poe, *Christian Witness in a Postmodern World*, 136.

who is calling them to respond in faith.[8] The personal testimony of healing, because it carries a certain epistemic authority, has a unique power to pave the way for the truth of the gospel.[9]

Summary and Conclusion:
Theological and Pastoral Considerations

For the many reasons outlined in the chapters above, we are now in a position to conclude strongly that healing plays an *indispensable role* in the proclamation of the gospel. The relationship between healing and evangelization in the Scriptures is so significant that any serious biblically-based effort to evangelize postmodern culture needs to consider integrating prayer for physical healing into the preaching of the gospel.

Some readers perhaps will acknowledge the validity of the exegetical insights in the above chapters but might not be as ready to accept the implications that these insights entail. Perhaps this lack

---

8. Johnson, *When Heaven Invades Earth,* 127.

9. It should be noted that while healing carries an epistemic authority in postmodern culture, not all aspects of Western culture would be so open to miracles. This is particularly true in various areas of academia where modern Enlightenment rationalism—with its ideological offspring scientism and naturalism—still have a significant influence on the minds of many today. After all, according to rationalism, faith in miracles is foolish since miracles *cannot* happen. Thus, many fallen-away Catholics and those outside the church steeped in such a worldview would have a serious difficulty in believing that miracles, in fact, do happen. Perhaps part of the reason why faith in healing is increasing is that we are in a postmodern world that does not rule out *a priori* such events from happening. Nevertheless, people holding to a modern worldview still strongly resist the *fact* of miraculous healings. Unfortunately, a rationalist resistance to the gospel of word and deed is still present in the academic world of biblical studies, where many scholars often succumb to the demythologization of the miracles of Jesus and the disciples. Approaching the Scriptures in this way prevents scholars (and their students) from believing that miracles still happen today. The resultant unbelief in turn disables them from considering the critical role miracles can play in the preaching of the gospel. Nevertheless, the power of experiencing even one healing miracle of Jesus in the preaching of the gospel is powerful enough to blow down the rationalist house of cards and eventually lead one to faith in Jesus.

of acceptance was understandable in a foregone era of the church, when healing was not as prominent and effective in evangelization as it is today. In the contemporary experience of the church's life, the efficacious prayer for physical healing is one of the major reasons why charismatic/Pentecostal churches are experiencing explosive growth all over the world.[10] Thus, given the urgent task of evangelization before the church today, it is no longer acceptable to set aside the distinctive role that healing plays in confirming, demonstrating, and expressing the gospel to those who hear it. As we conclude this study, we will discuss four theological and pastoral considerations in the church's efforts to reintegrate the dimension of healing in her efforts to fulfill the new evangelization.

First, one of the recurring insights that is woven throughout this book is the remarkable unity of word and deed in the proclamation of the gospel. The gospel of the kingdom that Jesus and the disciples preach is not simply a message of fact; it is a message of power that is demonstrated or expressed through the working of deeds that serve as signs of the reality preached: salvation. The unity of word and deed is especially clear in Luke 4, where Jesus' messianic mission to evangelize explicitly includes both words and deeds. O'Reilly is correct when he understands that Jesus' word, like that of the Old Testament prophets, has two parts: the *dionetic* (the intelligible content of the message) and the *dynamic* (the power of the word to effect change). Or, in other language, we can say the word of the gospel is not simply informative, it is also *performative*.[11] The deeds of healing and deliverance that characterize

10. For more on the role of healing and the expansion of charismatic/Pentecostal churches see Botha, "The New Reformation: the Amazing Rise of the Pentecostal-Charismatic Movement in the 20th century," 295-325; Keener, *Miracles*; Browne, *Global Pentecostal and Charismatic Healing*; Clark, *Evangelism Unleashed*; and Anderson, *To the Ends of the Earth*. For examples of healing and evangelization in the Catholic Church, see the testimonies from around the world in Part III of Pontifical Council for the Laity and ICCRS, *Prayer for Healing*, and the ministry of Damian Stayne, www.coretlumen-christi.org.

11. Ratzinger, "Difficulties in Teaching the Faith Today," 69. Christianity has always understood that the spoken word of the gospel has the capacity to effect change in the present. This truth, which underlies the church's theology of the

the ministries of Jesus and the disciples serve not only to validate the truth of the message preached, but also to express and make present in a provisional way the very reality that is preached. The combination of the preached word expressed in deed presents the truth in a tangible way that enables the hearers to respond to the message in faith.

As the mission of Jesus is continued in and through the church, both in the commissioning accounts in the Gospels and in Acts, we find the two-part gospel intact: the church's bold preaching is accompanied by signs, wonders, and healings. The *theological foundation* for the permanent power transfer needed for this anointed mission of the early church is described in a special way in Acts, where the disciples are baptized in the Spirit at Pentecost. Receiving the same Spirit that Jesus received, the disciples do what Jesus did. According to the Pauline letters, we discover that the gospel comes in demonstration of the Spirit and power, in which signs of healing serve as *convincing proof* of the gospel. Yet these deeds that serve as signs to accompany the preaching of the word in Paul do not merely function as extrinsic demonstrations of the truth of the gospel preached; in a mysterious way, they *form an intrinsic part of that very gospel*, as seen in Paul's description of the gospel in terms of word and deed in Romans 15. Nowhere in Scripture is there an indication that the gospel will at some point no longer need deeds to accompany the preached word. Therefore, when we examine the proclamation of the gospel in light of the deeds that accompany them, we are unable to establish neat and logical distinctions, either in fact or in theory, between the word of the gospel and the deeds that act as signs of that gospel.

---

sacraments, can be applied analogously to the preached word and the signs that follow. What Cardinal Ratzinger says in his essay on catechesis therefore can apply to the unity of word and deed in the preaching of the gospel: "The gospel is more than (good) 'news'. It is (glad) 'tidings,' or a 'message' that, as the contemporary philosophy of language puts it, has not only an informative but also a 'performative' effect, which means that it intends to intervene in the existential situation of the listener and to change it; only when this has happened has the message 'arrived' or been received at all." (Ibid., 69.)

Second, the dual nature of the proclaimed gospel seems to be closely related theologically to the dual nature of divine revelation as taught by the Second Vatican Council; they both have a sacramental structure. The council fathers understood that the plan of salvation is revealed in both deeds and words that have an inner unity.

> This plan of revelation is realized by deeds and words having an inner unity: the deeds wrought by God in the history of salvation manifest and confirm the teaching and realities signified by the words, while the words proclaim the deeds and clarify the mystery contained in them. By this revelation then, the deepest truth about God and the salvation of man shines out for our sake in Christ, who is both the mediator and the fullness of all revelation.[12]

According to Francis Martin, the mutual illumination of words and deeds in the plan of divine revelation here in *Dei verbum* can be referred to as the "sacramentality of revelation."[13] Thus, divine revelation in its very nature in history has a *sacramental* structure in that God reveals himself in words and deeds.[14] If this is true, then it seems that the *proclamation* of that revelation should have a similar sacramental structure precisely in order that

12. Second Vatican Council, *Dei verbum*, n.p.

13. Martin, "Revelation and Its Transmission," 57.

14. Avery Dulles also speaks of the sacramental structure of revelation in terms of words and deeds. "The attesting word of revelation is never a piece of abstract theory nor is it a mere report about empirical facts. Rather, it is the self-expression of a person caught up in the dynamism of God's saving action . . . As an event in the history of salvation, the proclamation of God's word is both a demand and a grace. Like a sacramental action, the word of God effects what it signifies. The symbolic or sacramental structure of revelation is impressively, though very concisely, indicated in Vatican II's Constitution *Dei verbum*. Revelation is seen as a loving approach whereby God mysteriously emerges from His silence and invites His beloved creatures to enter into fellowship with Himself. 'This plan of revelation is realized by deeds and words having an inner unity: the deeds wrought by God in the history of salvation manifest and confirm the teaching and realities signified by the words, while the words proclaim the deeds and clarify the mystery contained in them.'" Dulles, "The Symbolic Structure of Revelation," 72–73.

people of every age can have the opportunity to respond to that revelation in faith.[15] A sacramental structure of the preaching of the gospel is, in fact, what we discover as we examine the New Testament data: the word of the gospel, from Jesus to Paul, is accompanied by deeds.[16] Of course, the deeds that accompany the gospel do not consist solely in deeds of healing; there are other deeds that ought to accompany the preaching of the gospel in Scripture.[17] Nevertheless, deeds of healing in the New Testament seem to constitute an essential component of this proclamation. Moreover, if evangelization in the New Testament is considered paradigmatic for the evangelization of the church at all times, then the surest way for the church to maximize the intended response of repentance and faith is for the preaching of the gospel to retain its sacramental form and include deeds of healing.[18]

15. In his dissertation on the theology of revelation of Avery Dulles, Abraham Fisher suggests that God can communicate revelation to a person through the personal experience of miraculous healing. Such events are "revelatory symbols" communicated to individuals who receive them in the context of a community which gives the authoritative interpretation for that revelation. Fisher, *The Church as Symbolic Mediation*, 228.

16. In addition to the life of the church (in the Scriptures and the sacraments) and the interior witness of the Spirit within the disciples, Francis Martin believes that the "works" and miracles of the disciples constitute a "third mode" of the Spirit's witnessing concerning Jesus and making him known. Martin, "The Spirit of the Lord is Upon Me," 71.

17. Various works of love and mercy are examples of other indispensable deeds that correspond to the word that is preached.

18. This is not to say that evangelization cannot be successful without signs of healing, especially since healing is only *one* of the indispensable signs of the inbreaking kingdom that expresses the gospel. Rather, the point is that if according to the New Testament the *surest* way to maximize the response of repentance and faith when preaching the gospel is to ensure its sacramental form by including signs of healing, then the church today can maximize its evangelistic effectiveness by following more closely the biblical model and seeking to include healing alongside its preaching. This point is valid even if historically the presence of healing in the preaching of the *kerygma* has not always been normative. A possible fruitful area for further research beyond the scope of this book would be an examination of the extent to which successful Catholic evangelization included signs of healing in various times and contexts in Church history. Such a study would be fascinating and enlightening

This leads us to an important question. If the proclamation of the gospel in Scripture is *sacramental* in that it involves the unity of words and deeds (of healing), then by virtue of what can the contemporary church claim it does not need powerful signs that correspond to the truth of the gospel? It seems that, at the very least, a most effective way to preach the gospel is to preach the way Jesus did: through words, and deeds of healing that accompany the word. While there are all kinds of deeds that act as signs of the coming of the kingdom, healings occupy a unique place in the New Testament as signs that reveal and convince people of the truth of the gospel. It is quite significant that healings, which make up the majority of the miracles that accompany the gospel in the New Testament, are not arbitrary signs to confirm the message's divine source. Healings are perhaps the most *sacramental* of all of the signs that can accompany the preaching of the gospel. As visible signs, healings make present and point to God's ultimate purpose for man: his salvation from the destruction of sin and death and the gift of the fullness of life with God in eternity.[19] In this way, the message of the gospel with signs of healing makes present the mystery of Christ himself and points, in a most fitting way, to God's purposes for man.[20] When people living in a pluralistic and skeptical culture experience or witness the inbreaking of God's kingdom through signs of healing, they are confronted with the absolute truth of God's love in Christ in a way that is difficult to deny. This confrontation, because it points beyond itself, has the power to break people free from their philosophical and spiritual malaise and give them a new possibility of responding to God in Christ. If bringing people to a decision to follow Jesus is the goal

---

but may or may not bolster the biblical argument of this book.

19. Montague, *The Holy Spirit*, 153.

20. Pope Benedict XVI, *Jesus of Nazareth*, 176. Healing is so central to God's purpose for man that God identifies himself as Israel's healer in the episode of God making the bitter water sweet in wilderness: "I am the Lord, your healer."(Ex 15:26) This declaration identifies God as one who heals, restores, and makes whole fallen man. God reveals himself as mankind's healer. Thus, when Jesus and his disciples heal they are revealing and making present God's purposes for mankind.

of evangelization, then the signs of healing that accompany the gospel can play a crucial role in leading people in the postmodern world to such a decision.

Our third point is that many in the church, in order to see people healed, need an *increase of faith* in Jesus' desire and power to heal as they proclaim the gospel. Perhaps one of the reasons why many in the church are not seeing the signs of healing in their evangelization is a simple lack of faith which translates into no one praying for the sick. Commenting on Mark 16:18, Randy Clark observes,

> Pay attention to the fact that *signs are to follow those who believe*. Are we today not *those who believe*? The words of Scripture include not only those who believed in the days of the first apostles and the early church, but to believers throughout the ages. If the commission to preach the gospel is still in effect for believers today, the sign that we shall lay hands on the sick and the sick will recover is also still in effect.[21]

Laying hands on the sick and seeing them recover is a sign that Jesus says will accompany and confirm the preaching of the gospel (Mark 16:20). Does the church still believe that Jesus desires to heal today?[22] The healings of the disciples did not just spontaneously happen as they proclaimed the gospel. Rather, the disciples actually had to step out in faith and exercise the authority Jesus entrusted to them in order to heal the sick.[23] That there

21. Clark, *Power to Heal*, 45.

22. Cardinal Suenens challenges Catholics: "We must renew within ourselves that faith in the power of the Lord to act in favour of the sick person. We should not be too hesitant in learning from examples of living faith that we see among our Protestant brothers . . . Often we are afraid to believe who in fact we really are—that is to say, we are hesitant to believe in the Christ who lives and acts within us. We do not dare believe in prayer which can include miracles." Suenens, *A New Pentecost?*, 52–53.

23. Like Jesus, the disciples in Acts heal the sick in various ways. They heal by *command* (Acts 3:6; 9:34; 14:10; 22:16), by announcement (Acts 9:17 and 20:10), and by the laying on of hands (Acts 5:12; 9:40; 14:3; 28:8). God also uses Peter's shadow (Acts 5:15) and Paul's handkerchiefs to heal people (Acts 19:11–12).

are no physical healings recorded in the New Testament without human mediation testifies to this fact.[24] If the disciples' ministry is modeled after Jesus', as the Gospels and Acts suggest, then the disciples had to intentionally step out in faith to heal the sick.

If this is true, then the faith necessary for healing in the context of preaching the gospel does not consist simply of the belief that God *can* heal people sovereignly as one preaches the gospel. Rather, the faith for healing must consist of the belief that God *wants* to heal and include the *actual stepping out in faith* to pray with someone for healing. Therefore, the Christian who wishes to bring the power of healing into his evangelization must (1) learn how to pray for healing, (2) preach that Jesus still heals today so as to stir up faith in Jesus' power to heal, and then (3) *demonstrate that faith* by actually praying with people for them to be healed.[25] How do Christians know they have the faith for God to heal in their evangelization? The answer is simple: they are in fact praying with the sick for healing in Jesus' name. The Lord who confirms the message of his messengers with signs needs his messengers to give him the opportunity to do so. Only in this way can healing play the significant role in evangelization today that it did in the New Testament.

Finally, the new evangelization cannot be successful without returning to the source of evangelization: the power of the Holy Spirit. Throughout the New Testament the disciples are only capable of fulfilling the mission Jesus gives to them because he bestows upon them the power of the Holy Spirit. Without the church returning to the upper room of Pentecost, there cannot be a new evangelization. John Paul II said as much at the dawn of the new millennium:

---

24. Clark, *Global Awakening Ministry Team Manual*, 45.

25. Resources on teaching and equipping the church for the ministry of healing are on the rise: Francis MacNutt, *The Practice of Healing Prayer: A How-To Guide for Catholics*; Mary Healy, *Healing: Bringing the Gift of God's Mercy to the World*; and most recently Damian Stayne, *Lord Renew Your Wonders: Spiritual Gifts for Today*. Some other very helpful resources are Randy Clark, *Global Awakening Ministry Team Training Manual* and *Power to Heal*.

> Over the years, I have often repeated the summons to
> the *new evangelization.* I do so again now, especially in
> order to insist that we must rekindle in ourselves the
> impetus of the beginnings and allow ourselves to be
> filled with the ardour of the apostolic preaching which
> followed Pentecost.[26]

The call to rekindle in the church the impetus of the beginnings is a call to be filled anew with the Holy Spirit for the urgent
task before us.[27] In her commentary on Mark 16:14–18, Mary
Healy applies John Paul II's summons to healing: "Part of this
impetus must include a renewed understanding of the role of healings and miracles in the work of evangelization."[28] Since the Spirit
who gives the ardor to proclaim the gospel at Pentecost is the same
Spirit who gives the disciples power to perform miracles in Jesus'
name, the church has the *theological foundation* to integrate healing into the new evangelization.

If in the sacraments of baptism and confirmation a Christian
receives the same Spirit who anointed Jesus, then each Christian
already possesses the *spiritual power* to carry out the demanding
task of preaching the gospel and praying for the sick effectively.
The graces given in these sacraments, unfortunately, often need
to be renewed and personally appropriated in what some scholars
of the charismatic renewal call the "baptism in the Holy Spirit."[29]
When the graces of these sacraments are unleashed in people's
lives, God moves in mighty ways as they preach the gospel. Unfortunately, many Christians for various reasons have reduced the
working of miracles to an *optional spirituality* that one is free to

26. John Paul II, *Novo Millenio Ineunte*, n.p.

27. Many are unaware that recent popes have been continuously calling for
the Church to pray for a new Pentecost. Just as the first evangelization would
not have happened without the first Pentecost, the new evangelization cannot
and will not happen without a new Pentecost to empower it. For a discussion
on the popes and the call for a new Pentecost see Martin, *A New Pentecost.*

28. Healy, *Gospel of Mark,* 334.

29. For a more detailed theological explanation of the grace of the sacraments and their personal appropriation see the Doctrinal Commission of
ICCRS, *Baptism in the Holy Spirit.*

accept or reject.[30] As a result, the utilization of the Spirit's power for healing is left to a few specialists in renewal movements and the practice of healing prayer is relegated to the periphery of the church's evangelization efforts.

In light of the impending demographic crisis facing the church today in which large portions of Christians are no longer practicing the faith—with many more leaving every day—leaders in the church need to set aside an outdated biblical theology and reawaken their faith that the miracle power of the Spirit is still available today and is therefore not optional in evangelization. Randy Clark observes,

> We need the power of the Holy Spirit; it is not an evangelical side-item. It should *not* be a topic of theological debate. Paul expressly states that it was not rhetoric and words alone that brought his listeners to faith in Christ. Rather, he presents the true source of his evangelistic effectiveness as a demonstration of the Spirit's power in their midst.[31]

Perhaps one reason why the power for healing in the preaching of the gospel is often left to specialists and not integrated into the mission of each Christian is the existence of a theological tension in the New Testament. On the one hand, Jesus commands all his disciples, including the wider group of the seventy, to "heal the sick" and gives his authority to them to fulfill this command. Moreover, Jesus says that the sign of laying hands on the sick for healing will "accompany those who believe" (Mark 16:17). A biblical argument can be made that all Christians can pray efficaciously for the sick, even if our study confirms a particular link between healing and the preaching of the gospel. But on the other hand, the glimpse we are given into the Christian community at Corinth indicates that there are those with "charisms of healings" who are

---

30. As we have seen in our study, such a reduction is biblically and theologically unwarranted.

31. Clark, *The Essential Guide to the Power*, 181.

used as instruments of healing more than others, a teaching that is confirmed by the church.[32]

If most Christians do not believe that they possess the authority from Jesus to heal the sick, then only those who believe they do (or discover that they do) will pray for the sick. Moreover, only those who pray will see results. If this continues, the number of people who pray for the sick will always remain very low. But if Christians boldly believe that God wants to heal the sick and that Jesus gives the power to do just that, then they will likely seek the charism of healing from the Spirit and indeed receive it. Such faith in crying out for the Spirit bears the fruit of actually receiving more of the Spirit. Having received more, they will be more confident to go out and preach the gospel and pray for the sick, which will result in more healings. The theological tension between these two positions can find a resolution in Acts 4, where the apostolic church implores God for more of the Spirit for a more effective evangelization.

Like the persecuted apostolic church in Acts that implored God for more boldness and signs and wonders, the Catholic Church today must be stirred up in faith that *there is always more* of the Holy Spirit. The church must implore God to grant not only an increase of boldness in preaching the word, but also of signs, wonders, and healings to accompany the preaching. If the apostolic church was able to humbly recognize its poverty in the face of the enormous evangelical task before it and respond in faith by imploring God for the power necessary to accomplish that task, then the church of today can do the same and see similar results. In this sense, the church's prayer to God in Acts 4 can serve as a model for the contemporary church for integrating healing in the new evangelization. May the whole church confidently pray with Raniero Cantalamessa his prayer based on Acts 4:

> Lord turn your gaze upon us, today, also extend your hand so that cures, miracles, and wonders are performed in the name of Jesus, because we have become distracted, deaf, and hard of heart and the words no longer suffice. Let us have the courage again to ask you again for signs

32. *Catechism of the Catholic Church*, sec. 1508.

and prodigies not for us, but for your glory and for the spread of your kingdom . . . Our world is again—or has become once more—in great part unbelieving. For this reason we need some of your signs that might convince the world or at least reclaim its attention. You have promised us to work together with those who preach and to confirm their words "through accompanying signs" (Mark 16:20).[33]

33. Cantalamessa, *The Mystery of Pentecost*, 32.

Bibliography

Altrock, Chris. *Preaching to Pluralists: How to Proclaim Christ in a Postmodern Age.* St Louis: Chalice, 2004.

Anderson, Allen. *To the Ends of the Earth: Pentecostalism and the Transformation of World Christianity.* Oxford Studies in World Christianity. New York: Oxford University Press, 2012.

Beavis, Mary Ann. *Mark.* Paideia: Commentaries on the New Testament. Grand Rapids: Baker Academic, 2011.

Bell, R.H. "Demon, Devil, Satan." In *Dictionary of Jesus and the Gospels,* 2nd ed., edited by Joel B. Green and Jeanine Brown, 193–202. Downers Grove, IL: IVP Academic, 2013.

Blomberg, Craig. "Healing." In *Dictionary of Jesus and the Gospels,* edited by Joel B. Green and Scot McKnight, 299–306. Downers Grove, IL: InterVarsity, 1992.

Botha, Eugene. "The New Reformation: the Amazing Rise of the Pentecostal-Charismatic Movement in the 20th century." *Studia Historiae Ecclesiasticae* 33 (2007) 295–325.

Brown, Candy Gunther. *Global Pentecostal and Charismatic Healing.* New York: Oxford University Press, 2011.

Brown, Raymond. *The Gospel According to John 1–12: Introduction, Translation and Notes,* Anchor Bible 29. Garden City, NY: Doubleday, 1966.

———. *The Gospel According to John 13–21,* Anchor Bible 29a. Garden City, NY: Doubleday, 1970.

Bruce, F. F. *The Epistle to the Galatians: A Commentary on the Greek Text.* The New International Greek Testament Commentary Series. Grand Rapids: Eerdmans, 1982.

Cantalamessa, Raniero. *The Holy Spirit in the Life of Jesus.* Collegeville, MN: Liturgical, 1994.

———. *The Mystery of Pentecost.* Collegeville, MN: Liturgical, 2001.

Catechism of the Catholic Church. 2nd ed. Washington DC: United States Catholic Conference, 2000.

Bibliography

Cho, Youngmo. *Spirit and Kingdom in the Writings of Luke and Paul: An Attempt to Reconcile these Concepts.* Paternoster Biblical Monographs. Milton Keynes, UK: Paternoster, 2005.

Clark, Randy. *The Essential Guide to the Power of the Holy Spirit: God's Miraculous Gifts at Work Today.* Shippensburg, PA: Destiny Image, 2015.

———. *Evangelism Unleashed.* Mechanicsburg: Global Awakening, 2011.

———. *Global Awakening Ministry Team Training Manual.* Mechanicsburg, PA: ANGA, 2004.

———. *Power to Heal: Keys to Activating God's Healing Power in Your Life.* Shippensburg: PA, Destiny Image, 2015.

———. "Prayer for Healing." Presentation presented at the Voice of the Apostles Conference, Nashville, TN, August 2015.

Clark, Randy, and Bill Johnson. *The Essential Guide to Healing.* Minneapolis: Chosen, 2011.

Congar, Yves. *I Believe in the Holy Spirit.* Translated by Geoffrey Chapman. New York: Crossroad, 2000.

Congregation for the Doctrine for the Faith. "Instruction on Prayers for Healing." http://www.vatican.va/roman_curia/congregations/cfaith/documents/rc_con_cfaith_doc_20001123_istruzione_en.html.

Doctrinal Commission of the International Catholic Charismatic Renewal Services. *Baptism in the Holy Spirit.* Vatican City: ICCRS, 2012.

———. *Guidelines on Prayers for Healing,* rev. ed. Vatican City: ICCRS, 2012.

Dulles, Avery. "The Symbolic Structure of Revelation." *Theological Studies* 41 (1980) 51–73.

Dunn, James D. G. *The Acts of the Apostles.* Narrative Commentaries Series. Valley Forge, PA: Trinity International, 1996.

Fee, Gordon. *God's Empowering Presence: The Holy Spirit in the Letters of Paul,* Peabody, MA: Hendrickson, 1994.

Fisher, Abraham. "The Church as Symbolic Mediation: Revelation Ecclesiology in the Theology of Avery Dulles, S.J." PhD diss., 2013.

France, R. T. *The Gospel of Mark: A Commentary on the Greek Text.* Grand Rapids: Eerdmans, 2002.

Gallagher, Robert. "From 'Doingness' to 'Beingness': A Missiological Interpretation of Acts 4:23–31." In *Mission in Acts: Ancient Narratives in Contemporary Context,* edited by Robert Gallagher and Paul Hertig. New York: Orbis, 2004.

Garland, David. *1 Corinthians.* Baker Exegetical Commentary on the New Testament. Grand Rapids: Baker Academic, 2003.

Gorman, Michael. *The Apostle of the Crucified Lord: A Theological Introduction to Paul and His Letters.* Grand Rapids: Eerdmans, 2004.

Greig, Gary, et al. *The Kingdom and the Power: Are the Healing and the Spiritual Gifts Used by Jesus and the Early Church Meant for Today?* Ventura, CA: Regal, 1993.

Bibliography

Grundmann, Walter. "δύναμαι." In *Theological Dictionary of the New Testament*, eds. Gerhard Kittel, Geoffrey W. Bromiley, and Gerhard Friedrich, 284–317. Grand Rapids: Eerdmans, 1964

Hahn, Scott, ed. *Catholic Bible Dictionary.* New York: Doubleday, 2008.

Hansen, G. Walter. *Galatians.* IVP New Testament Commentary Series. Downers Grove, IL: InterVarsity, 1994.

Healy, Mary. *The Gospel of Mark.* Catholic Commentary on Sacred Scripture. Grand Rapids: Baker Academic, 2008.

———. *Healing: Bringing God's Gift of Mercy to the World.* Huntington, IN: Our Sunday Visitor, 2015.

Healy, Mary, and Peter Williamson. "Biblical Orientations for the New Evangelization." *The Urgency of the New Evangelization: Answering the Call,* Ralph Martin, 99-126. Huntington, IN: Our Sunday Visitor, 2013.

Hendrickx, Herman. *The Miracle Stories of the Synoptic Gospels.* New York: Harper Collins, 1988.

Hille, Rolf. "The Uniqueness of Christ in a Postmodern World and the Challenge of World Religions." Paper presented at the Lusanne Committee for World Evangelization Conference in Pattaya, Thailand, Sept. 29–Oct. 5, 2004. https://www.lausanne.org/wp-content/uploads/2007/06/LOP31_IG2.pdf.

International Catholic Renewal Services and Pontifical Council for the Laity, *Prayer for Healing: International Colloquium.* Rome: ICCRS, 2003.

Jewett, Robert. *Romans: A Commentary.* Hermeneia: A Critical & Historical Commentary on the Bible. Minneapolis: Fortress, 2007.

Johnson, Bill. *When Heaven Invades Earth: A Practical Guide to a Life of Miracles.* Shippensburg, PA: Destiny Image, 2003.

Keener, Craig. *Acts: An Exegetical Commentary: Introduction and 1:1–2:47.* Grand Rapids: Baker Academic, 2012.

———. *Gospel of John: A Commentary,* 2 vols. Peabody, MA: Hendrickson, 2003.

———. *Matthew.* IVP New Testament Commentary Series. Downers Grove, IL: InterVarsity, 1997.

———. *Miracles: The Credibility of the New Testament Accounts,* 2 vols. Grand Rapids: Baker Academic, 2012.

———. *Spirit Hermeneutics: Reading Scripture in Light of Pentecost,* Grand Rapids: Eerdmans, 2016.

———. *The Spirit in the Gospels and Acts: Divine Purity and Power.* Peabody, MA: Hendrickson, 1997.

Klappert, Bertold. "λόγος." In *The New International Dictionary of New Testament Theology,* edited by Colin Brown, 1081–1117. Grand Rapids: Eerdmans, 1986.

Kurz, William. *Acts of the Apostles.* Catholic Commentary on Sacred Scripture. Grand Rapids: Baker Academic, 2013.

Ladd, George. *Gospel of the Kingdom: Scriptural Studies in the Kingdom of God.* Grand Rapids: Eerdmans, 1959.

———. *The Presence of the Future,* rev. ed. New York: Harper & Row, 1974.

Bibliography

————. *A Theology of the New Testament,* rev. ed. Grand Rapids: Eerdmans, 1993.

MacNutt, Francis. *Healing,* rev. ed. Notre Dame: Ave Maria, 1999.

————. *The Practice of Healing Prayer: A How-To Guide for Catholics.* Frederick, MD: The Word Among Us, 2010.

Martin, Francis "Revelation and Its Transmission." In *Vatican II: Renewal Within Tradition,* edited by Matthew Lamb and Matthew Levering, 55–76. New York: Oxford University Press, 2008.

————. "'The Spirit of the Lord is Upon Me: The Role of the Holy Spirit in the Work of Evangelization." In *The New Evangelization: Overcoming the Obstacles,* edited by Steve Boguslawski and Ralph Martin, 59–82. New York: Paulist, 2008.

Martin, Francis, and William Wright. *The Gospel of John.* Catholic Commentary on Sacred Scripture. Grand Rapids: Baker Academic, 2015.

Martin, Ralph. *A New Pentecost.* Ann Arbor, MI: Renewal Ministries, 2011.

Matera, Frank. *New Testament Theology: Exploring Diversity and Unity.* Louisville: Westminster John Knox, 2007.

————. *Romans.* Paideia: Commentaries on the New Testament. Grand Rapids: Baker Academic, 2010.

Montague, George. *First Corinthians.* Catholic Commentary on Sacred Scripture. Grand Rapids: Baker Academic, 2011.

————. *The Holy Spirit: Growth of a Biblical Tradition.* Eugene, OR: Wipf & Stock, 2006.

Moore, Russell. *The Kingdom of Christ: The New Evangelical Perspective.* Wheaton, IL: Crossway, 2004.

Moraine, Jack. *Healing Ministry.* Choctaw, OK: HGM, 2010.

Morphew, Derek. *Breakthrough: Discovering the Kingdom.* Capetown, South Africa: Vineyard International, 1991.

Njiru, Paul. *Charisms and the Holy Spirit's Activity in the Body of Christ: An Exegetical-Theological Study of 1 Corinthians 12:4–11 and Romans 12:6–8.* Tesi Gregoriana, Serie Teologia 86. Rome: Gregorian University Press, 2002.

O'Reilly, Leo. *Word and Sign in the Acts of the Apostles: A Study in Lucan Theology.* Analecta Gregoriana 243. Rome: Editrice Pontificia Universita Gregoriana, 1987.

Parsons, Mikeal. *Acts.* Paideia: Commentaries on the New Testament. Grand Rapids: Baker Academic, 2008.

Peeters, Marguerite. *The New Global Ethic: Challenges for the Church.* Brussels: Institute for Intercultural Dialogue Dynamics, 2006.

Plummer, Robert. *Paul's Understanding of the Church's Mission: Did the Apostle Paul Expect the Early Christian Communities to Evangelize?* Paternoster Biblical Monographs. Milton Keynes, UK: Paternoster, 2006.

Poe, Harry. *Christian Witness in a Postmodern World.* Nashville: Abingdon, 2001.

Bibliography

Pope Benedict XVI. *Jesus of Nazareth: From the Baptism in the Jordan to the Transfiguration.* New York: Doubleday, 2007.

Pope John Paul II. "Novo Millenio Ineunte." https://w2.vatican.va/content/john-paul-ii/en/apost_letters/2001/documents/hf_jp-ii_apl_20010106_novo-millennio-ineunte.html.

Ratzinger, Joseph. "Difficulties in Teaching the Faith Today." In *Handing on the Faith in an Age of Disbelief,* edited by Joseph Ratzinger, et al. San Francisco: Ignatius, 2006.

Richardson, Alan. *The Miracle Stories of the Gospels.* New York: Harper and Brothers, 1941.

Ruthven, Jon. *What's Wrong with Protestant Theology?* Tulsa, OK: Word & Spirit, 2013.

Sawvelle, Bob. *A Case for Healing Today: A Biblical, Historical, and Theological View of Christian Healing.* Self-published, CreateSpace, 2014.

Second Vatican Council. *Dei verbum.* http://www.vatican.va/archive/hist_councils/ii_vatican_council/documents/vat-ii_const_19651118_dei-verbum_en.html.

Shelton, James. *Mighty in Word and Deed: The Role of the Holy Spirit in Luke-Acts.* Eugene, OR: Wipf & Stock, 2000.

Smith, James K. A. *Who's Afraid of Postmodernism?: Taking Derrida, Lyotard, and Foucault to Church.* Grand Rapids: Baker, 2006.

Smith, Thomas. "Postmodernism and the New Evangelization." www.f4ne.org/images/New_Evangelization_Research_Paper.doc.

Sri, Edward, and Curtis Mitch. *The Gospel of Matthew.* Catholic Commentary on Sacred Scripture. Grand Rapids: Baker Academic, 2010.

Stanley, David. "Salvation and Healing." *The Way* 10 (1970) 298–317.

Stayne, Damian. *Lord Renew Your Wonders: Spiritual Gifts for Today.* Frederick, MD: Word Among Us, 2017.

Stronstad, Roger. *The Charismatic Theology of St. Luke: Trajectories from the Old Testament to Luke-Acts,* 2nd ed. Grand Rapids: Baker Academic, 2012.

Suenens, Leon Joseph. *A New Pentecost.* Ann Arbor, MI: Servant, 1975.

Sullivan, Francis A. *Charisms and Charismatic Renewal: A Biblical and Theological Study.* Eugene, OR: Wipf & Stock, 2004.

Tarazi, Paul. *Galatians: A Commentary.* Orthodox Biblical Studies. Crestwood, NY: St Vladimir's, 1994.

Turner, Max. "Holy Spirit." In *Dictionary of Jesus and the Gospels,* edited by Joel B. Green and Scot McKnight, 341–51. Downers Grove, IL: InterVarsity, 1992.

———. *The Holy Spirit and Spiritual Gifts in the New Testament Church and Today,* rev. ed. Peabody, MA: Hendrickson, 1998.

Twelftree, Graham. *Paul and the Miraculous: A Historical Reconstruction.* Grand Rapids: Baker Academic, 2013.

———. "Signs, Wonders, Miracles." In *Dictionary of Paul and His Letters,* edited by Gerald F. Hawthorne, et al., 875–77. Downers Grove, IL: InterVarsity, 1993.

Bibliography

VanHoye, Albert. "Healings in the Life of Jesus and in the Early Church." In *Prayer for Healing: International Colloquium*, 34–47. Rome: ICCRS, 2003.

———. *I Carismi nel Nuovo Testamenti*. Analecta Biblica 191. Rome: Gregoriana & Biblical, 2011.

Wahlen, C. "Healing." In *Dictionary of Jesus and the Gospel*, 2nd ed., edited by Joel B. Green and Jeannine Brown, 362–70. Downers Grove, IL: InterVarsity, 2013.

Warrington, Keith. "Acts and the Healing Narratives: Why?" *Journal of Pentecostal Theology* 14 (2006) 189–217.

Wells, David. *Above All Earthly Pow'rs: Christ in a Postmodern World*. Grand Rapids: Eerdmans, 2004.

Wimber, John, and Kevin Springer. *Power Evangelism,* 2nd ed. Minneapolis: Chosen, 2009.